BLIZZARD'S
ACTION TOYS

BLIZZARD'S ACTION TOYS

Richard Blizzard

UNWIN

HYMAN

LONDON SYDNEY WELLINGTON

First published in Great Britain by the Trade Division of Unwin Hyman Limited, 1988.

Unwin Hyman Limited
15–17 Broadwick Street
London W1V 1FP

Allen & Unwin Australia Pty Ltd
8 Napier Street, North Sydney, NSW 2060, Australia

Allen & Unwin New Zealand Pty Ltd with the Port Nicholson Press
60 Cambridge Terrace, Wellington, New Zealand

ISBN 0-04-440131-0

Photography by Richard Smiles
Designed by John Grain
Artwork and typesetting by Quorum Technical Services Ltd
Printed by the Bath Press, Avon

ACKNOWLEDGEMENTS

A book is not just the work of the author, but the combination of a group of very talented people whose combined efforts eventually result in the end product 'the book'.

I am very grateful not only for professional advice but the encouragement and help I have received in compiling this volume of toys and models. So a very special 'thank you' to you all including:

Peter Farley, Stephanie Banks and Mervyn Hurford who were responsible for all the drawings and cutting lists.

Jenny Spring, who untangled heaps of untidy hand written notes to produce a legible script.

David Roscoe, Public Relations Director Vickers, for assistance with the boat-tailed racing Rolls Royce.

Max Kellert, Director I H Daimler-Benz Museum, Stuttgart, Germany, for assistance with the Blitzen Benz racing car.

Richard Ide, Malcolm Pitcher, Andrew Seacombe, Richard Kobberling and Horst W Keisler of M A N, who showed such enthusiasm for the trucks featured in this book and helped with photographs, plans and details — thank you all for your efforts on my behalf.

Peter Grimsdale and Jack Baird of The Swedish Finnish Timber Council whose help, advice and technical knowledge of timber have been invaluable.

Richard Smiles for photographs.

Robin Hyman, Mary Butler, Elizabeth Nicholson and Jane Elliot, who waited so patiently for the toys and models to be completed.

CONTENTS

INTRODUCTION

The Projects

INTRODUCTION

I have thoroughly enjoyed designing and making the collection of toys and models in this book. I have tried to create a range of toys that will give everybody an opportunity to get started and enjoy making toys.

I know from my post bag that one problem many woodworkers have is the supply of suitable timbers from which to create toys. I have therefore used Nordic Redwoods for many of the projects and have tried where ever possible to use stock size widths and, most important of all, thicknesses.

For children, play and work are one, and the toys we give or make for them are their tools. To adults child's play may seem trivial (and at some ages annoying) but to the child, play is a form of experiment and a most vital activity in the first five years of life. Through play children learn the most important basic skills of life – seeing, hearing, walking, talking, thinking and discovering something about themselves and the world they live in – skills on which all future learning is based.

Therefore with this in mind I have tried to give the young child lots of things to make play interesting. For instance the crane has moving jib pulleys and sand hopper, and the water trucks lift. The working mechanisms will give hours of fun and might just teach the adults something too! The traditional toys have not been missed and the toddler's trike with its trailer, the teddy bears' buggy and the bunk beds will give endless pleasure.

For the skilled woodworkers I have included the famous, beautifully streamlined Blitzen Benz racing car, and the MAN articulated tractor and, for those of you who like modelling, a boat-tailed 2-seater sporting Rolls Royce.

Children love playing, but playing with a toy that has been made by someone they know and love is something very special for both child and maker. So don't worry what your child will say to your first woodworking efforts – they will be thrilled and so will you.

I hope you will have as much pleasure from the toys and models in this book as I have had in making them.

Richard Blizzard 1987

TEDDY BEARS BUGGY

(See colour plate 1)

When I was a child there was a limited number of soft toys that one could buy and so I naturally became very attached to my teddy bear (I've still got him). Today there is a great variety of soft cuddly toys available in a range of beautiful colours, so to make sure that they all get an outing I have built this sturdy buggy.

This is a good project for a beginner and will last many years.

TIMBER
The timber is 'stock size' Finnish Redwood (not usually red in colour) so it's easily available.

TO MAKE
1.   Make a start by cutting the sides, ends and base to length. Before any shaping is started, pencil in on the inside edges of the sides the position of the base and the ends.

2.   As the ends are at an angle to the base, carefully mark on to the bottoms of each end the necessary angle. The angle is then planed. It is best to do this working from both sides, otherwise if you just plane straight across it will split the end grain and completely spoil the wood. This is the only tricky job to be achieved in making the buggy. Now the ends are ready for assembly.

3.   Tape the two sides together and drill the axle holes. Now the sides have to be cut to shape — if you don't have a jigsaw, a coping saw will do this job but obviously it will take a little longer. Once the cutting out has been done the saw blade marks can be removed with a spokeshave. You will find that candle wax rubbed on the sole of the spokeshave will make the job much easier.

4.   Such is the strength of modern glues that no traditional joints are necessary, the base ends and sides are simply glued together. However before putting any glue on to the wood, assemble the job

dry, following the pencil lines made and check that everything lines up. It is also useful to slip the axles into the holes as this is an added guide.

Where wood actually meets wood I always 'key' the surface with my Stanley knife. Keying is simply cutting into the wood with a criss-cross pattern. This allows the wood glue to get a better hold on the wood fibres and makes an even stronger joint. Obviously the keying needs to be made inside the pencil lines otherwise you will have some very ugly knife marks in just the wrong places.

When you are sure everything lines up, glue the 'body' together. A weight placed on the sides will be sufficient to help the glue bond to the wood. As the glue is liquid there will be a tendency for the parts to move slightly for the first 5 minutes, so keep an eye on the job to make sure that the pieces stay in place.

5.   Now find two suitable lengths of timber for the handles, and taping them together drill the hole at the top for the handle (it's best to first obtain the dowel rod before drilling) and the holes for the screws that attach the handles to the sides. Once the holes have been drilled then take off the tape and remove the saw cuts with a spokeshave.

6.   The screw holes holding the handles to the sides are counterbored which enables the screw head to go below the surface of the wood and allows a wood plug to be glued in. This method removes all traces of ugly wood screws and gives a much more pleasing finish.

Now glue the dowel rod (or piece of broom handle) into the handles and attach to the side of the buggy.

7.   The axle rods are steel and need a chamfer filed on their ends to allow the spring caps to fit. Thread the axles through the holes and fit the wheels on. On my prototype I felt a touch of colour would improve the job so I painted the wheel rims yellow with a band of red on the outside.

Teddy Bear's Buggy Cutting List

Sides	2 off 432 × 191 × 20mm (17 × 7½ × ¾in) timber
Head	1 off 197 × 184 × 20mm (7¾ × 7¼ × ¾in) timber
Foot	1 off 197 × 171 × 20mm (7¾ × 6¾ × ¾in) timber
Base	1 off 324 × 197 × 20mm (12¾ × 7¾ × ¾in) timber
Handle Support	2 off 350 × 44 × 20mm (13¾ × 1¾ × ¾in) timber
Handle	1 off 273mm (10¾in) × 22mm (⅞in) diam dowel
Ancillaries	4 off 143mm (5⅝in) diam moulded wheels
	2 off 356mm (14in) × 9mm (⅜in) diam steel axles
	4 off 9mm (⅜in) spring dome caps

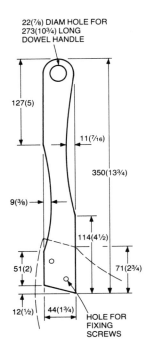

22(⅞) DIAM HOLE FOR
273(10¾) LONG
DOWEL HANDLE

127(5)

11(⁷⁄₁₆)

350(13¾)

9(⅜)

114(4½)

51(2)

71(2¾)

12(½)

44(1¾)

HOLE FOR
FIXING
SCREWS

HANDLE SUPPORT
MAKE TWO

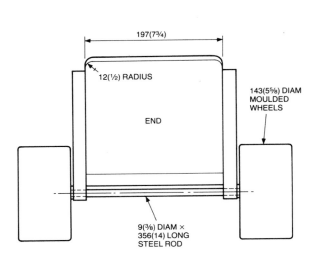

197(7¾)

12(½) RADIUS

END

143(5⅝) DIAM
MOULDED
WHEELS

9(⅜) DIAM ×
356(14) LONG
STEEL ROD

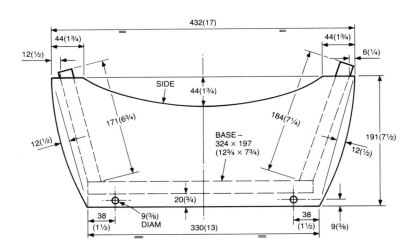

432(17)

44(1¾)

12(½)

SIDE

44(1¾)

44(1¾)

6(¼)

171(6¾)

184(7¼)

191(7½)

12(½)

12(½)

BASE –
324 × 197
(12¾ × 7¾)

20(¾)

38
(1½)

9(⅜)
DIAM

330(13)

38
(1½)

9(⅜)

NOTE:
ALL TIMBER 20(¾) THICK

BODY ASSEMBLY

SCOOTA TRIKE

(See colour plate 2)

Toddlers who have discovered the joys of going where they want to, soon look for a means of transport to get there faster. So begins the very real danger of being mortally wounded in your hall or living room, and the process of instilling into the young road hog that some rules have to exist for the safe passage of other household users. Eventually garden paths or park walkways come to the rescue as you persuade the toddler that they are not mere paths, but ring roads! From then on all is well, (apart from a few decapitated flowers) and the only noise is that of an offspring, pretending to be an articulated lorry complete with sound effects, trundling up and down the path.

TIMBER
The timber used is Nordic Redwood.

TO MAKE
1. Make a start with the chassis. Mark out carefully and drill all the necessary holes for the seat, but leave the large hole that takes the steering rod until later. A large piece of wood runs full length beneath the seat which gives this little trike great strength. Glue the wood on to the underside of the seat and secure it at the front end with a screw. You will see from the drawing that all the screws are counterbored with wood plugs glued on top, which not only protects a child's leg and bottom from scratches but gives the toy a far better finish.

2. The back axle block has to be cut out. As few of us have a drill of sufficient length to go right through from one side it is necessary to cut out the radialized piece in the middle of the axle block. Having carefully marked both ends of the axle block, drill in from both ends, making sure to keep the drill at 90 degrees in both planes. This method avoids the need for a very lengthy and expensive wood bit.

3. The axle block is now attached to the back vertical piece which is in turn glued and screwed to the seat and the cross piece under the seat. Even if you don't intend to make a trailer it's a good idea to fit a hitch (youngsters always want to pull something along even if it's the tea trolley!). The hitch itself wants to be just as big and strong as possible and is glued into the hitch assembly base. The whole unit is now glued and screwed on to the underside of the back axle unit.

4. The front wheel steering block is now marked out and the first job is to drill the axle and steering rod hole. Once these holes have been drilled, shape off the top edge. Now drill and cut to shape the steering bar and top fixing 'collar'. The purpose of the collar is to fix the steering bar in place and take some of the 'play' out of the steering gear. Ideally all the steering joints should be stiff as these will slacken up after the first 1,000 miles! If you find that these joints slacken up badly after use then a few coats of varnish will remove this problem. Glue the steering bar on to the shaft.

5. The back is now shaped and both glued and screwed on to the rear of the trike. Screw heads are covered by wood plugs.

6. The axles are cut to length and chamfers filed on to the ends. Before fitting the wheels I painted a band of red around the wheel rims adding a touch of colour. The wheels are now put on and the spring caps fitted to keep them in place.

TRAILER
A trike is fun but far more playable with if it can take things to and fro. This little trailer is very strong and constructed like a box with the top missing.

TO MAKE
1. Cut the ends, sides and the base to length. Now drill all the necessary counterbore holes. Glue and screw the ends to the base first. Now check that the sides will fit and if there is any overhang, plane flush with the base. The sides are now glued and screwed in place.

2. The trailer hitch is cut to length and a large hole bored to take the hitch pin from the trike. It is important that this hole is oversize which will allow uneven ground to be traversed. The hitch is glued and screwed on to the underside of the base.

3. The axle is held in place by two wood blocks. Mark out and drill the blocks for the axle and the screw fixing holes. Cut the axle to length and after chamfering the ends, thread the blocks on to the axle. Now position the blocks on the underside of the trailer and glue and screw in place. Push the wheels on and fit the spring caps.

Scoota Trike Cutting List

Chassis Assembly	1 off 438 × 191 × 20mm (17¼ × 7½ × ¾in) timber
	1 off 406 × 60 × 44mm (16 × 2⅜ × 1¾in) timber
	1 off 191 × 178 × 20mm (7½ × 7 × ¾in) timber
Axle Block	1 off 191 × 51 × 20mm (7½ × 2 × ¾in) timber
Seat Back	1 off 191 × 178 × 20mm (7½ × 7 × ¾in) timber
Hitch Assembly	1 off 191 × 102 × 20mm (7½ × 4 × ¾in) timber
	1 off 89mm (3½in) × 22mm (⅞in) diam dowel
Steering Column Assembly	1 off 254 × 44 × 41mm (10 × 1¾ × 1⅝in) timber
	1 off 152 × 86 × 44mm (6 × 3⅜ × 1¾in) timber
	1 off 35 × 35 × 32mm (1⅜ × 1⅜ × 1¼in) timber
	1 off 235mm (9¼in) × 22mm (⅞in) diam dowel
Ancillaries	4 off 143mm (5⅝in) diam road wheels
	1 off 203mm (8in) × 9mm (⅜in) diam steel front axle
	1 off 298mm (11¾in) × 9mm (⅜in) diam steel axle
	4 off 9mm (⅜in) spring dome caps

Trike Trailer Cutting List

Floor	1 off 254 × 191 × 20mm (10 × 7½ × ¾in) timber
Side Walls	2 off 292 × 197 × 20mm (11½ × 7¾ × ¾in) timber
Front and Rear	2 off 197 × 191 × 20mm (7¾ × 7½ × ¾in) timber
Tow Bar	1 off 254 × 41 × 41mm (10 × 1⅝ × 1⅝in) timber
Axle Blocks	2 off 64 × 41 × 41mm (2½ × 1⅝ × 1⅝in) timber
Ancillaries	2 off 143mm (5⅝in) diam road wheels
	1 off 337mm (13¼in) long × 9mm (⅜in) diam steel axle
	2 off 9mm (⅜in) spring dome cap

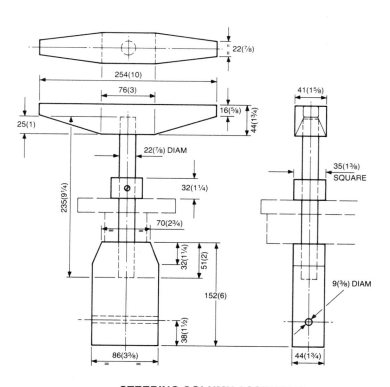

STEERING COLUMN ASSEMBLY

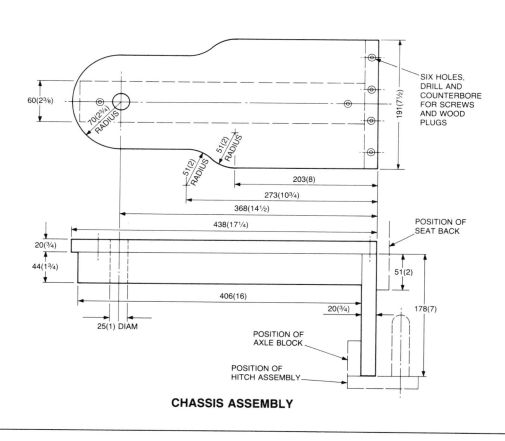

CHASSIS ASSEMBLY

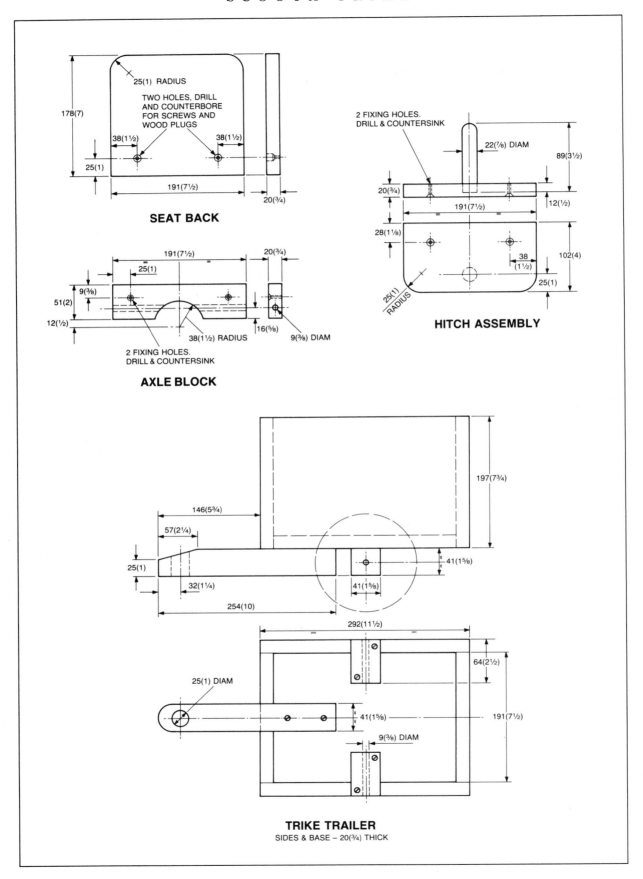

SEAT BACK

25(1) RADIUS

TWO HOLES, DRILL
AND COUNTERBORE
FOR SCREWS AND
WOOD PLUGS

178(7)

38(1½)   38(1½)

25(1)

191(7½)

20(¾)

AXLE BLOCK

191(7½)   20(¾)

25(1)

9(⅜)

51(2)

12(½)

38(1½) RADIUS   16(⅝)   9(⅜) DIAM

2 FIXING HOLES.
DRILL & COUNTERSINK

HITCH ASSEMBLY

2 FIXING HOLES.
DRILL & COUNTERSINK

22(⅞) DIAM

89(3½)

20(¾)   12(½)

191(7½)

28(1⅛)

38
(1½)

102(4)

25(1)
RADIUS   25(1)

TRIKE TRAILER
SIDES & BASE – 20(¾) THICK

197(7¾)

146(5¾)

57(2¼)

25(1)

32(1¼)   41(1⅝)

254(10)   41(1⅝)

292(11½)

64(2½)

25(1) DIAM

41(1⅝)   191(7½)

9(⅜) DIAM

BUNK BEDS FOR TEDS

(See colour plate 3)

The Teddy Bear has found a special place in the affections of most children (and some adults) and the arrival of a new, particularly friendly brown bear, and the need to accommodate him prompted the making of these bunk beds.

This is a good project for woodworking 'first time' as no joints are required, only the careful gluing and screwing together of sides and ends.

TIMBER

The wood is Finnish Redwood which is easily obtainable at builders merchants and relatively knot-free.

TO MAKE

1. Start by marking out all the ends and sides. Don't forget to allow for the width of the saw cut when the measurements are made. Once the marking out is done over the pencil lines with a marking knife and 'scribe' the lines in deeply. By using this method the timber will cut without leaving ragged ends.

2. The boards are 'butt jointed'. This simply means that the sides are glued on to the ends. Butt jointing relies entirely on the glue holding the joint and I therefore recommend that in addition the pieces are all screwed together. To avoid the ugly screw head showing I used a plug cutter which is a very useful addition to any tool box. Plug cutters can be bought as a set — one tool to actually cut the plug the other to counterbore the hole for both the screw and plug to fit into.

Once all the ends and sides have been cut, the holes for the screws and the plug should be bored. The plugs are cut from pieces of waste wood.

3. To allow the bears to get into bed easily the sides are recessed, this can easily be cut out using a coping saw. Saw tooth marks can be removed with glasspaper.

4. With the ends and sides cut to length and the screw holes bored the actual assembly can begin. The sides are glued on to the ends. Use a good wood glue and put plenty of adhesive on the end grain as this absorbs adhesive. It is obviously helpful to have two cramps to hold the pieces together. If you don't have cramps then it is easier to assemble it one joint at a time. The screws need to be done up tightly which will have the effect of pulling the glued butt joints together. Once all the screws are in firmly check the bunk bed for 'squareness'. Now glue the wooden plugs over the ends of the screws, and once the glue is dry trim off the plugs 'flush' with the sides. Then glue the plywood bases in place.

5. The two bunks are held together by four lengths of wood. These are attached by screws. Once again counterbore the screw holes and cut wood plugs. Now glue and screw the four lengths of wood on to the bunks.

6. The ladder is not difficult to make providing that you:

- Tape together two lengths of wood.
- Mark the position of the rungs.
- Drill the holes for the rungs.
- Cut the dowels that form the rungs accurately to length, chamfer off each rung end very slightly as this will help when assembling the ladder.
- Remove the tape from ladder sides and after putting a spot of glue on each rung (dowel) end fit all the rungs into one side. Now assemble the second side on to the rungs. It can be a little difficult getting started but once the rungs are in, put the ladder in the vice and squeeze the sides together.

The ladder is now screwed to the sides of the bunks.

Bunk Beds for Teds Cutting List

Vertical Supports	4 off 396 × 44 × 22mm (15⅝ × 1¾ × ⅞in) timber
Sides	4 off 432 × 143 × 20mm (17 × 5⅝ × ¾in) timber
Ends	4 off 178 × 143 × 20mm (7 × 5⅝ × ¾in) timber
Bases	2 off 432 × 218 × 3mm (17 × 8½ × ⅛in) plywood
Ladder Stringers	2 off 394 × 20 × 20mm (15½ × ¾ × ¾in) timber
Ladder Rungs	7 off 69mm (2¾in) × 6mm (¼in) diam dowel

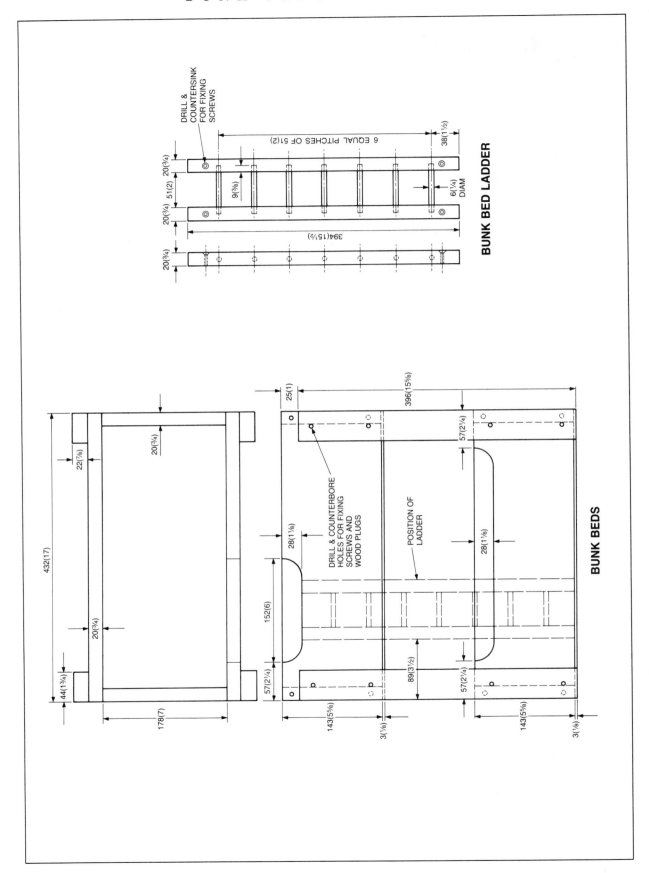

BUNK BED LADDER

BUNK BEDS

8

WILF

(See colour plate 4)

Sometimes when I look at my garden plants after a night of rain I find that something has eaten them. Could there just be some large plant eating creature with a friendly face lurking in the South West of England – someone like Wilf?

You can make as many body sections to this beastie as you like provided that you remember to add wheels to every other body section.

TIMBER
The timber used is Nordic Redwood.

TO MAKE
1. From the different grids given, mark out on to a cardboard template the different sized body sections. After cutting the shapes out transfer them on to a length of knot free plank. Knots are all right but avoid them at the jointed sections.

2. Cutting out the different pieces can be done with a coping saw or jigsaw. Once all the sections have been cut out remove all the saw marks.

3. Jointing the different pieces together you will require some sort of clamping device – ideally a vice. Fit the sections to be jointed in the vice and with a wood boring bit in the drill, carefully drill the hole. Don't force the drill through or you will make an ugly hole at the bottom. Repeat this operation for all sections.

4. To make sure the toy articulates properly it is necessary to chamfer carefully around all the joints. It is vital to have smooth edges here to prevent any pinched fingers.

5. To give a little 'body' to the beast, offcuts of wood are glued along the tops of each section. Ears are cut out and attached to the head piece only.

6. The antennae are made from offcuts and holes drilled to take the plastic covered curtain wire.

A note of caution – all children put things in their mouths – so be very careful that you glue the antennae to the curtain wire with epoxy resin glue; if in doubt, leave the antennae off all together.

7. Such a large beastie requires a fairly wide wheel base, so spacers are fitted either side of the legs. Before fitting the legs it's important to drill the axle holes.

8. Cutting wooden wheels is not as difficult as you may think. Mark out very carefully with a compass, and before starting fit a new blade in the coping saw! If you have marked out the wheels on a plank it's easier to drill the axle holes before the wheels are cut.

If cutting out wheels is too daunting a task then you can buy a set of tank cutters.

9. Before assembling the wheels rub candle wax on to the axles, but be careful to avoid the areas to be glued.

10. The hand grip is an offcut of dowel rod – one end is fixed in the beastie's mouth, the other left free to pull it along.

11. The eyes need to be stuck into the head using epoxy resin glue. Many different colours and sizes of eye can be bought from shops which stock materials for soft toy making. Be warned – *fix the eyes in well* – and check every day that they are still firmly attached.

Wilf Cutting List

Head	1 off 300 × 200 × 20mm (12 × 8 × ¾in) timber
	2 off 225 × 100 × 20mm (9 × 4 × ¾in) timber
	2 off 100 × 50 × 20mm (4 × 2 × ¾in) timber
Eyes	2 off 20mm (¾in) × 9mm (⅜in) diam dowel
1st Body	1 off 300 × 200 × 20mm (12 × 8 × ¾in) timber
	2 off 150 × 75 × 20mm (6 × 3 × ¾in) timber
2nd Body	1 off 300 × 200 × 20mm (12 × 8 × ¾in) timber
	2 off 125 × 50 × 20mm (5 × 2 × ¾in) timber
3rd Body	1 off 275 × 175 × 20mm (11 × 7 × ¾in) timber
	2 off 150 × 50 × 20mm (6 × 2 × ¾in) timber
Tail	1 off 200 × 150 × 20mm (8 × 6 × ¾in) timber
	2 off 125 × 50 × 20mm (5 × 2 × ¾in) timber
Pivot Pins	4 off 76mm (3in) × 6mm (¼in) diam dowel
Body Antenna	4 off 60 × 25 × 12mm (2⅜ × 1 × ½in) timber
Head Antenna	2 off 75 × 25 × 12mm (3 × 1 × ½in) timber
Ear	2 off 138 × 50 × 20mm (5½ × 2 × ¾in) timber
Legs	6 off 175 × 150 × 20mm (7 × 6 × ¾in) timber
Wheel Spacers	6 off 25 × 25 × 20mm (1 × 1 × ¾in) timber
Wheels	6 off 108mm (4¼in) diam × 20mm (¾in) thick timber
Axles	3 off 138mm (5½in) × 9mm (⅜in) diam dowel
Hand Grip	1 off 102mm (4in) × 16mm (⅝in) diam dowel
Bit	1 off 102mm (4in) × 12mm (½in) diam dowel
Ancillaries	1 off 500mm (20in) length of nylon card
Antenna	Make from 625mm (25in) long plastic covered curtain wire

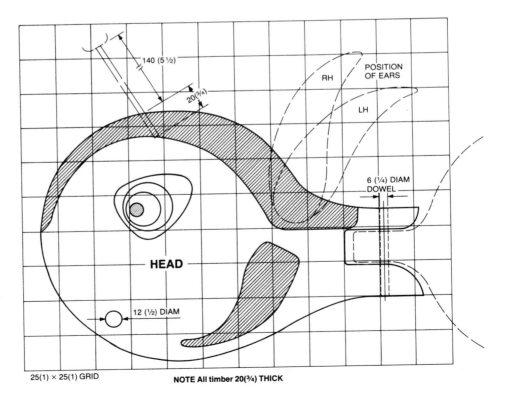

SHADED AREAS CUT FROM 20 (¾) TIMBER AND GLUED TO BOTH SIDES OF HEAD, BODY AND TAIL

140 (5½)

20(¾)

POSITION OF EARS

RH

LH

6 (¼) DIAM DOWEL

HEAD

12 (½) DIAM

25(1) × 25(1) GRID

NOTE All timber 20(¾) THICK

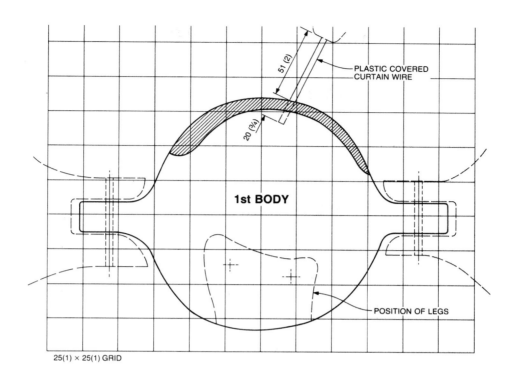

1st BODY

51 (2)

20 (¾)

PLASTIC COVERED
CURTAIN WIRE

POSITION OF LEGS

25(1) × 25(1) GRID

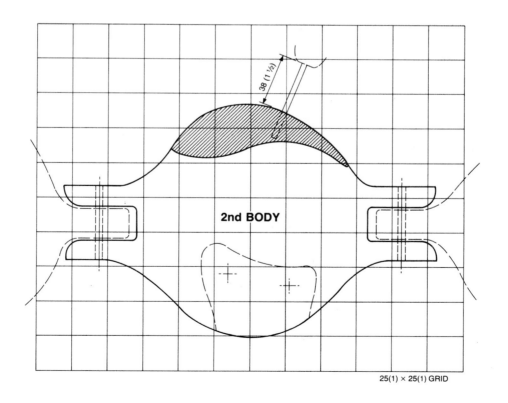

2nd BODY

38 (1 ½)

25(1) × 25(1) GRID

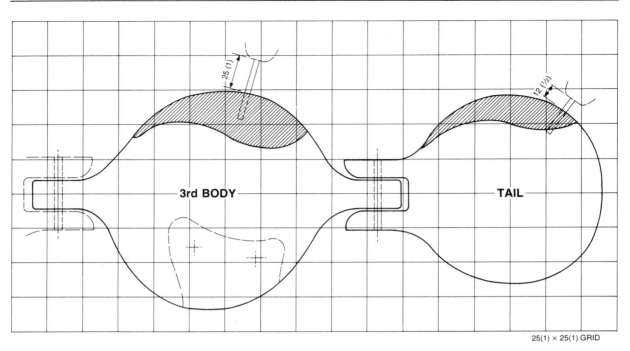

3rd BODY

TAIL

25 (1)

12 (½)

25(1) × 25(1) GRID

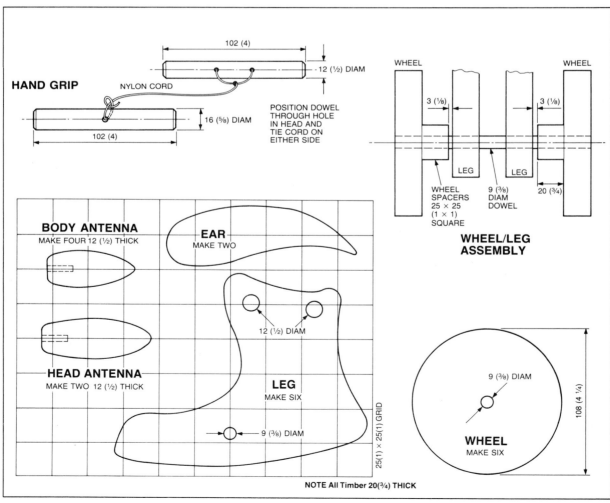

HAND GRIP

102 (4)

12 (½) DIAM

NYLON CORD

16 (⅝) DIAM

102 (4)

POSITION DOWEL
THROUGH HOLE
IN HEAD AND
TIE CORD ON
EITHER SIDE

WHEEL

WHEEL

3 (⅛)

3 (⅛)

LEG

LEG

WHEEL
SPACERS
25 × 25
(1 × 1)
SQUARE

9 (⅜)
DIAM
DOWEL

20 (¾)

**WHEEL/LEG
ASSEMBLY**

BODY ANTENNA
MAKE FOUR 12 (½) THICK

EAR
MAKE TWO

HEAD ANTENNA
MAKE TWO 12 (½) THICK

12 (½) DIAM

LEG
MAKE SIX

9 (⅜) DIAM

25(1) × 25(1) GRID

9 (⅜) DIAM

108 (4 ¼)

WHEEL
MAKE SIX

NOTE All Timber 20(¾) THICK

1909 BLITZEN-BENZ

(See colour plate 5)

The inspiration to build this car came from visiting the Mercedes museum at Stuttgart. Anyone who is interested in the history of transport should have the opportunity to look at the amazing collection of machines. You don't have to be a car 'buff' to appreciate this museum which has some of the most ingenious and beautiful cars I have ever seen.

The 1909 Blitzen-Benz set the seal on a sporting image that had grown since 1908. The streamlining of this car is very beautiful. From the beak-nosed radiator at the front, the line of the car flows through to the pointed tail at the back.

The shaping of the car is very difficult to specify with exact dimensions. We have given you the basis to work from, but quite obviously there is a great deal of planing and careful paring of wood to attain the Perfect shape.

TIMBER
The timber used is Brazilian Mahogany.

TO MAKE
1. The chassis is the first thing to make. To achieve a sense of curvature, pieces are glued onto the outside edges and chamfered off towards the engine compartment. Once these two outer pieces have been glued in place the chassis is clamped together and the position of the cross pieces marked.

Both chassis sides are held together by cross pieces that are stub morticed and tenoned into the longitudinal members. The mortice at the front of the chassis must be very carefully cut as the chassis is tapered just after this joint and forms part of the front spring arrangement.

When the mortices have been cut and the shaping at the front finished, drill the hole at the rear of the chassis to take the tie rod and then glue the chassis together.

2. For simplicity the springs on this model don't actually work as with the boat-tailed Ghost but are formed from pieces of wood. When the shaping of each spring has been completed these do look quite effective. Drill the axle holes for each spring and glue the front springs onto the chassis. The back springs are attached later.

3. The front axle is another example of the car maker's skill in forging axle beams – fortunately it is not so difficult in wood! A coping saw will cut out the initial shape but after that you need to use a chisel and glasspaper to round off all the edges. Very careful drilling of the axle hole is necessary.

4. The underbody is now marked out and shaped. A hole is drilled to take the rear drive shaft, and another at the front to take the cranking handle shaft. You may wish to use a large drill bit to remove a great deal of the unwanted wood in the middle of the underbody which will reduce the weight. The underbody has three 'cut outs' (which locate over the chassis cross members) and is glued into position when all shaping has been done.

5. The cranking handle is now made and, to get it to rotate smoothly in the underbody (crank case) a liberal application of candle wax is applied to the shaft.

6. One of the special features of this machine, the unique radiator, must now be shaped. A piece of black ribbed plastic is fitted into the centre, with small strips of wood glued down the two sides and along the bottom. The beaked part of the radiator needs a great deal of painstaking work, involving a little shaping before you offer it up to the front.

The radiator when finished is glued onto the recess that is cut at the front of the underbody.

7. The superstructure is formed from 3 pieces of wood – 2 sides, 1 top and a block that is glued onto the back. Begin by cutting out the driver's compartment in the top (bonnet) section. It's not necessary to cut out the driver's access point in the side piece yet. Now glue the bonnet onto the sides.

Cut and fit the engine bulkhead and dashboard, not forgetting to drill a hole for the steering wheel column.

Now cut a rebate in the block of wood that fits at the back. Studying the drawing carefully you can see that the top section has a 'lip' at the back into which the rebated block fits. Cut and fit the back floor pan which fits under the driver's seat. This forms the basic superstructure which now needs to be shaped.

Shaping begins by cutting the outer line of the bodywork. This shape is clearly shown in the plan view. If you have a bandsaw you will find this basic roughing out process quite easy, if not then a spokeshave is a good alternative. The basic shape of the block at the back can be cut using a handsaw. At this early stage cut out the driver's access at the side.

Once the correct curvature of the sides has been achieved, planing and spokeshaving of the bonnet can begin. It is vital to offer up the work continually to the radiator at the front as you go along. The shaping cannot be carried out in isolation to the rest of the work.

The block at the back needs to be worked on from all angles – keep the job as even as possible from all sides and avoid cutting, planing or chiselling large chunks off any one part.

The crew compartment is shaped with a small gouge and a chisel. Round off all the edges paying particular attention to the dashboard region. This needs to be chiselled back into a nice smooth curve.

8. The cooling vents are made from thin strips of ash (or other contrasting coloured wood). These are glued onto strips of wood that are in turn glued onto the sides of the engine compartment. Make sure that room is left for the engine strap. A touch of realism is added by paring them to shape with a sharp chisel. Because the vents are so thin it's easiest to glue the vents onto their mounting block first, and then carry out final shaping.

9. The exhaust block and ports are now made. The tubing, painted black, is fitted into pre-drilled holes. Don't forget to cut out a notch for the belt which runs beneath the exhaust block.

10. The strap holding the bonnet in place is made from a watch strap and buckle. The ends of the straps are lengthened by gluing on some additional lengths of leather strip.

11. The gear lever, hand-brake and quadrants are made. These are fixed to the side of the car using a raised head chrome-plated screw. They don't actually work, but they look the part.

12. The cockpit is now 'fitted out'. Once the woodwork is in place it looks very good trimmed out in leather. A finely skived (thin) leather is used which is surprisingly easy to work. I found that a visit to my local shoe repair shop was the answer. I was able to buy not only the leather but the glue that the shoe mender uses. I find that it's best to cut paper templates before cutting the leather. Press the cardboard around the cockpit first and in this way you get a very clear impression of what the shape is. Folding a strip of leather around the cockpit is not difficult if you have the leather adhesive for the job. Don't be afraid to experiment – it's a real challenge and nothing looks as good as real leather.

13. The steering wheel is now made and fitted.

14. Now assemble the back springs and the drive chain assembly. The back springs are fixed to the chassis in two places – at the back by a rod that passes right through the spring and chassis on both sides, at the front by chrome-plated raised head screws. Once this is done the back axle is fitted.

I must admit to some extravagance, in that I bought four very expensive sprockets and, using a real miniature chain, fitted the spring links to complete the drive chain assembly. The sprockets were considerably more expensive than the chain so it's quite feasible to cut plywood sprockets to use with the chain which would save a great deal of expense.

15. The superstructure is held to the chassis by four screws which pass up through the underside.

16. The standard red disc wheels just don't look right, so I painted them with aluminium paint which is a great improvement.

17. You will find it is always easier to apply varnish before the wheels and drive shafts are assembled. For this particular model I used a satin finish Evode varnish – three coats rubbed down with a very fine glasspaper between each application and finished off with wax polish.

1909 Blitzen-Benz Cutting List

Body – Sides	2 off 378 × 67 × 20mm (14⅞ × 2⅝ × ¾) timber
– Top	1 off 384 × 107 × 25mm (15⅛ × 4³⁄₁₆ × 1in) timber
– Rear Cone	1 off 98 × 86 × 79mm (3⅞ × 3⅜ × 3⅛in) timber
– Floor	1 off 83 × 73 × 9mm (3¼ × 2⅞ × ⅜in) timber
– Rear Bulkhead	1 off 83 × 57 × 38mm (3¼ × 2¼ × 1½in) timber
– Seat	1 off 79 × 47 × 12mm (3⅛ × 1⅞ × ½in) timber
– Seat Back	1 off 79 × 28 × 12mm (3⅛ × 1⅛ × ½in) timber
– Dashboard	1 off 67 × 22 × 12mm (2⅝ × ⅞ × ½in) timber
– Front Bulkhead	1 off 67 × 64 × 3mm (2⅝ × 2½ × ⅛in) timber
Chassis – Longitudinal	2 off 483 × 20 × 12mm (19 × ¾ × ½in) timber
– Shapers	2 off 279 × 20 × 6mm (11 × ¾ × ¼in) timber
– Cross Members	4 off 76 × 20 × 12mm (3 × ¾ × ½in) timber
Under Body	1 off 311 × 64 × 51mm (12¼ × 2½ × 2in) timber
Front Spring	2 off 143 × 21 × 12mm (5⅝ × ¹³⁄₁₆ × ½in) timber
Rear Spring	2 off 127 × 38 × 12mm (5 × 1½ × ½in) timber
Front Axle	1 off 146 × 60 × 20mm (5¾ × 2⅜ × ¾in) timber
Starting Handle	1 off 25 × 12 × 6mm (1 × ½ × ¼in) timber
	1 off 57mm (2¼in) × 6mm (¼in) diam dowel
	1 off 25mm (1in) × 6mm (¼in) diam dowel
Steering Wheel	1 off 8mm (⁵⁄₁₆in) × 41mm (1⅝in) diam timber
	1 off 38mm (1½in) × 6mm (¼in) diam dowel
Radiator	1 off 98 × 54 × 51mm (3⅞ × 2⅛ × 2in) timber
	1 off 73 × 51 × 6mm (2⅞ × 2 × ¼in) timber
	1 off 51 × 6 × 3mm (2 × ¼ × ⅛in) timber
Cooling Vent	2 off 127 × 22 × 3mm (5 × ⅞ × ⅛in) timber
	Make from 1016 × 3 × 1.5mm (40 × ⅛ × ¹⁄₁₆in) timber
Exhaust	1 off 127 × 25 × 18mm (5 × 1 × ¹¹⁄₁₆in) timber
Quadrant	1 off 32 × 32 × 3mm (1¼ × 1¼ × ⅛in) timber
Gear Lever	1 off 76 × 9 × 3mm (3 × ⅜ × ⅛in) timber
Handbrake Lever	1 off 76 × 11 × 3mm (3 × ⁷⁄₁₆ × ⅛in) timber
Ancillaries	4 off 102mm (4in) diam road wheels
	1 off 215mm (8½in) × 9mm (⅜in) diam steel rear axle
	1 off 165mm (6½in) × 9mm (⅜in) diam steel drive shaft
	4 off 9mm (⅜in) spring dome caps
	2 off 64mm (2½in) × 6mm (¼in) diam steel front axles
	4 off 6mm (¼in) spring dome caps
	1 off 146mm (5¾in) × 5mm (³⁄₁₆in) diam steel rear spring pin
	2 off 5mm (³⁄₁₆in) spring dome caps
	4 off 17 tooth sprockets
	2 off 6mm (¼in) pitch chain × approx. 267mm (10½in) long
	2 off 3mm (⅛in) × 20mm (¾in) %diam × 9mm (⅜in) ⅟diam spacer
	1 off 73 × 47 × 3mm (2⅞ × 1⅞ × ⅛in) black ribbed plastic
	Make from 102mm (4in) × 6mm (¼in) %diam black tubing exhaust pipes

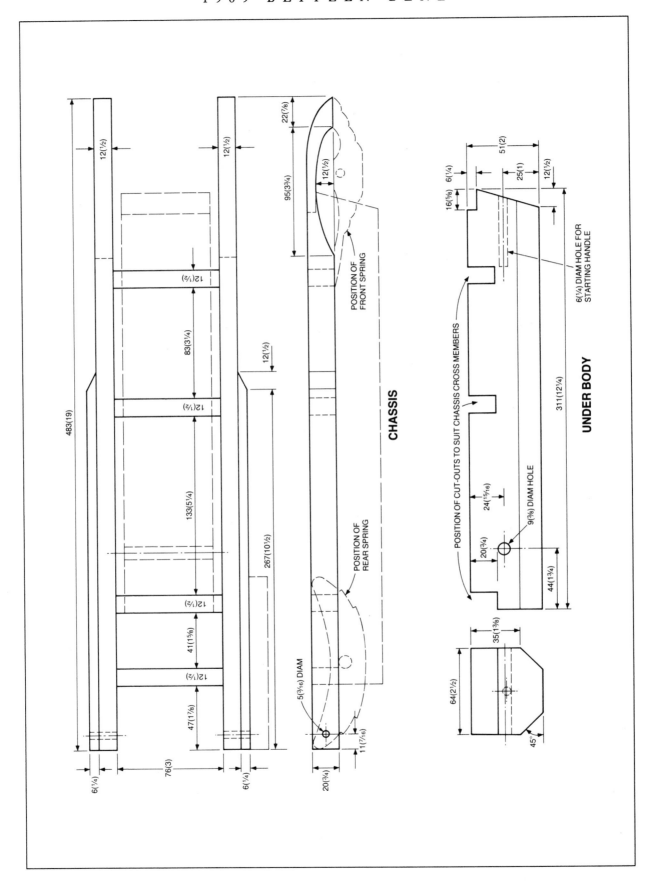

CHASSIS

UNDER BODY

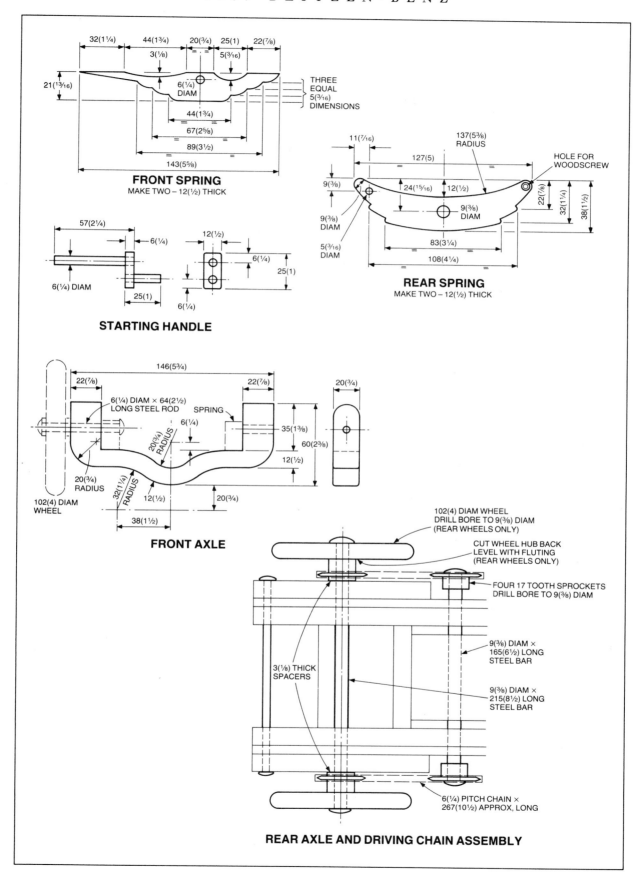

FRONT SPRING
MAKE TWO – 12(½) THICK

REAR SPRING
MAKE TWO – 12(½) THICK

STARTING HANDLE

FRONT AXLE

REAR AXLE AND DRIVING CHAIN ASSEMBLY

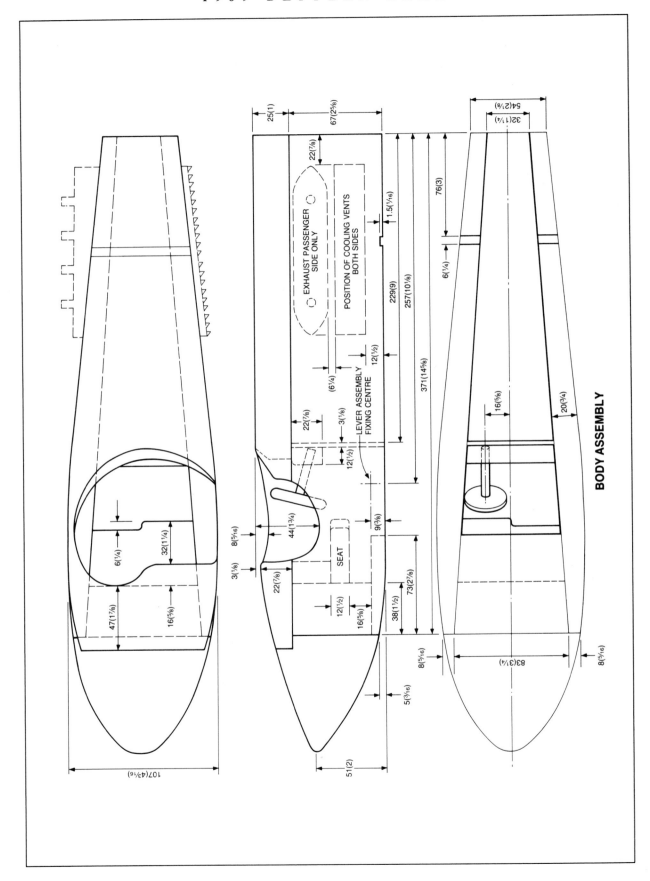

BODY ASSEMBLY

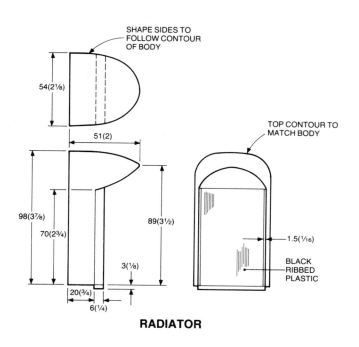

RADIATOR

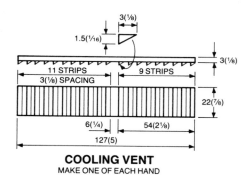

COOLING VENT
MAKE ONE OF EACH HAND

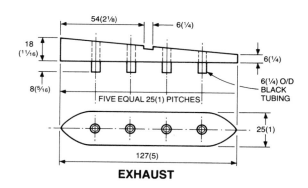

EXHAUST

**STEERING WHEEL
ASSEMBLY**

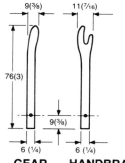

**GEAR
LEVER** **HANDBRAKE
LEVER**

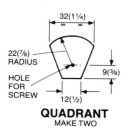

QUADRANT
MAKE TWO

3(⅛) THICK

GERMAN FOKKER TRIPLANE

(See colour plate 6)

In one of my earlier toy making books I built the legendary Sopwith Camel and became intrigued with the various aeroplanes of the First World War. It was therefore quite natural for me to build this competitor to the Sopwith. I have tried to give the wings a canvas-like appearance while scalloped trailing edges give the machine a character all of its own.

This aeroplane was extraordinarily agile in the air and could turn very quickly in flight, making it a very dangerous adversary to approach. For the historians among you the Red Baron never had an all red plane, only stripes of red were used.

The project is good for a beginner as it doesn't take too long to make and no difficult joints are needed.

TIMBER
The timber used is Nordic Redwood.

TO MAKE
1. Start by cutting out the fuselage. The slot at the bottom takes the wing and the one at the back the tail plane. The cockpit is cut out and a hole drilled to take the machine gun handle.

2. Shape up the two parts of the engine cowl and glue them onto the sides. Drill the hole to take the fixing screw for the propeller.

3. The wings are not difficult if you are systematic. Cut top, middle and bottom wings to length. Using clamps (or tape) fix the wing section very firmly together and having marked the positions of the dowel rods, drill the dowel rod holes. It is very important that none of the wing sections move in the drilling operation.

4. Once all the holes have been drilled the 'cut outs' have to be cut. Pencil a mark on each wing so that you can get them in the correct order once all the tapes have been removed.

Now work can begin on the cut out sections at the back of each wing. If you have a coping saw you will find it does a good job. Once all this cutting is complete wrap a piece of glasspaper round a dowel rod and remove the saw marks. Cut the six dowel rods that hold the wings to exactly the same length. Chamfer all the dowel rod ends slightly. Pencil mark on each rod the exact position of the centre wings. Now assemble the wings by gluing the dowel rods into the bottom wing first. 'Feed' the mid half wings into the dowel rods and tap them in place with a hammer (use a waste piece of wood under the hammer head). Getting the mid half wings exactly in the right place is important. Now

position the top wing, tapping it firmly on to the dowel rods.

You will find that the glue which has to be placed in each hole will tighten the movement of the wings very rapidly, so there is not much time to get things sorted out before the glue sets. It is therefore vital to have everything ready *before you start*.

5. The propeller is not too difficult to shape and make realistic. Drill the hole for the screw. I found a spokeshave very useful for removing the majority of wood and then finished off the job with glasspaper. You will find that two cap washers fitted between the prop and one under the screw head will give a good turn of speed.

6. The main undercarriage is now made. First cut all the pieces to length. Now cut rebates, (L-shaped grooves) on the top and bottom pieces which gives a good strong joint. The undercarriage ends are now drilled to take the axle hole. Glue the main undercarriage together.

7. The rear undercarriage seat and tail fin are now made. Prepare the wood for the seat and undercarriage and fix them together with tape. Now drill the holes for the dowel rods, taking care not to drill right through onto the top side of the seat.

The shaping of these two pieces can be done together. Now separate the two pieces and drill a hole in the centre of the rear undercarriage to take the castor wheel.

The whole assembly is fitted to the fuselage by screws, however these screw holes are counter-bored (the screw head set below the surface) and wooden plugs fitted over the tops of the screws. Prepare the holes but don't fit the unit yet.

Now glue the seat-back onto the seat, and cut out the fin, but once again don't glue it in place yet.

8. The machine guns are now made from two different sizes of dowel rod. Holes are drilled into the ends of the larger dowels and the small dowels glued into the larger. To give a 'good fixing' plane 'flats' on the sides of both of the larger dowels, then glue together ready for final fixing to the fuselage.

9. The machine gun rattle, or if you prefer the engine noise, comes from a clicker wheel. Mark out very carefully with a pencil making sure to drill the central hole before attempting to cut out the cogs. The clicker handle and clicker are now shaped up. A block is now fixed onto the side of the chassis to increase the 'bearing area' of the handle.

10. Now all parts are made final assembly can begin:

- Fix the wing section to the fuselage with glue and screws.

- Fix the machine guns, clicker handle, wheel and clicker lever into place.

- The clicker lever needs to fall lightly on the cog to give the right noise.

- Fix the rear undercarriage, seat and fin in place. The wooden pegs should be glued over the tops of the screw and when the glue is dry trimmed flush with the seat.

- The main undercarriage is now glued on to the bottom wing. When the glue is dry fit the axle and wheels. Remember to chamfer the ends of the steel rod, otherwise the spring caps will not fit.

- The most exciting job of all – fit the propeller – paying particular attention to the cup washers.

- Fit the small castor wheel at the back.

11. I think well finished wood does not need painting, however a few parts painted red can enhance the wood and as a suggestion: red prop, centre axle, machine guns, and wheel centres will set the plane off well.

German Fokker Triplane Cutting List

Fuselage	1 off 571 × 121 × 20mm (22½ × 4¾ × ¾in) timber
Engine cowl	2 off 121 × 22 × 20mm (4¾ × ⅞ × ¾in) timber
Reinforcing block	1 off 25 × 25 × 20mm (1 × 1 × ¾in) timber
Machine gun	2 off 32mm (1¼in) × 9mm (⅜in) diam. dowel
	2 off 76mm (3 in) × (1 in) diam. dowel
Top and bottom wing	2 off 559 × 121 × 20mm (22 × 4¾ × ¾in) timber
Mid-half wing	2 off 260 × 121 × 20mm (10¼ × 4¾ × ¾in) timber
Wing struts	6 off 254mm (10in) × 12mm (½in) diam. dowel
Propeller	1 off 356 × 44 × 20mm (14 × 1¾ × ¾in) timber
Main undercarriage	2 off 292 × 89 × 20mm (11½ × 3½ × ¾in) timber
	2 off 127 × 89 × 20mm (5 × 3½ × ¾in) timber
Clicker handle	1 off 51 × 25 × 20mm (2 × 1 × ¾in) timber
	1 off 133mm (5¼in) × 12mm (½in) diam. dowel
	1 off 76mm (3 in) × 12mm (½in) diam. dowel
Fixing block	1 off 25 × 25 × 20mm (1 × 1 × ¾in) timber
Clicker wheel	1 off 44 × 44 × 20mm (1¾ × 1¾ × ¾in) timber
Clicker lever	1 off 64 × 20 × 20mm (2½ × ¾ × ¾in) timber
Seat and rear undercarriage	2 off 229 × 121 × 20mm (9 × 4¾ × ¾in) timber
Rear undercarriage struts	4 off 146mm (5¾in) × 12mm (½in) diam. dowel
Seat back	1 off 229 × 117 × 20mm (9 × 4⅝ × ¾in) timber
Tail fin	1 off 275 × 150 × 20mm (11 × 6 × ¾in) timber
Ancillaries	
	2 off 152mm (6in) diam. wheels
	1 off 406mm (16in) × 9mm (⅜in) diam. steel axle
	2 off 9mm (⅜in) spring dome caps
	1 off 51mm (2in) diam. castor wheel assembly
	Assorted countersunk screws and cup washers

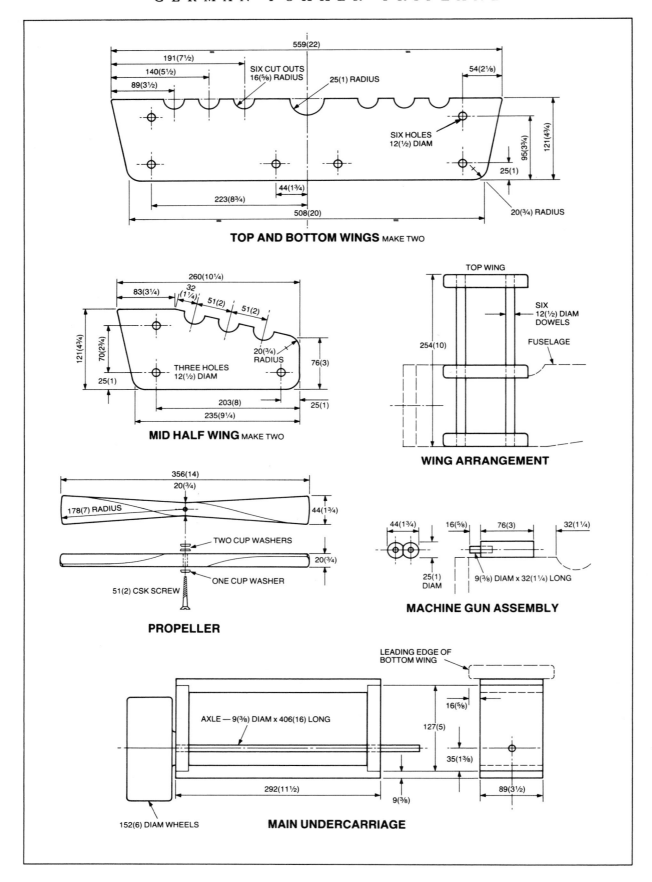

TOP AND BOTTOM WINGS MAKE TWO

MID HALF WING MAKE TWO

WING ARRANGEMENT

PROPELLER

MACHINE GUN ASSEMBLY

MAIN UNDERCARRIAGE

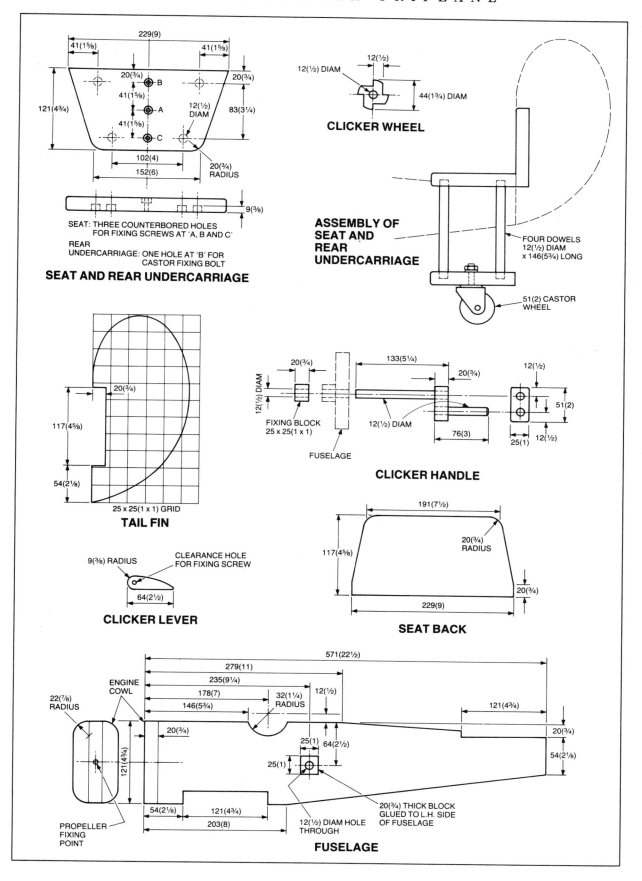

SEAT AND REAR UNDERCARRIAGE

SEAT: THREE COUNTERBORED HOLES FOR FIXING SCREWS AT 'A, B AND C'
REAR UNDERCARRIAGE: ONE HOLE AT 'B' FOR CASTOR FIXING BOLT

CLICKER WHEEL

ASSEMBLY OF SEAT AND REAR UNDERCARRIAGE

TAIL FIN

25 x 25 (1 x 1) GRID

CLICKER HANDLE

CLICKER LEVER

SEAT BACK

FUSELAGE

VOLVO LUXURY COACH

(See colour plate 7)

The luxury touring coach of today has come a long way from the 'charabancs' of the 1920s. These vehicles are now the motoring expresses of the 1980s, and can offer a high degree of luxury, full air conditioning being just one of their many features.

I have tried in this design to create a toy that has sufficient strength to withstand a youngster sitting (or standing) on the roof but enough interior detail to give an air of luxury.

It is not difficult to make and is a toy I have often been asked to design.

TIMBER
The coach is made from Nordic Redwood and has details picked out in a contrasting timber, in this case Brazilian mahogany.

TO MAKE
1. Make a start by cutting out the chassis. Once this is done drill the axle holes.

2. It is best to mark out the side panels as a pair. Cut out the driver's side window. This is done by drilling a hole, taking the coping blade out of one end of the frame, threading it through the hole and re-attaching it at the other side. The window is now cut out.

The side windows are much easier; as there is no bar along the top of the windows it's just a case of cutting the windows out with the coping saw. The wheel arches are now cut. A good deal of effort must now be put into cleaning all the saw cut marks off windows and wheel arches. I am fortunate to have a router and using a cutter I added a slight recess to all the window edges and wheel arches – this is not essential but it looks really good. Now make the rear panel and slightly chamfer off the bottom edge.

3. The coach floor has two functions:
    ● supporting the seats
    ● holding the sides together
The sloped section at the front has two 45 degree angles planed on to the ends and the adjoining section of the driver's floor a corresponding angle planed on it.

4. At the preparatory stage to gluing up, pencil clear lines on to the inside panels to give 'lining up' points. Once the wood has glue on the edges it's quite slippery and it does help tremendously if you have a line to follow and check once the cramps have been attached.

5. The sides are glued to the base at the same time that the floor is glued into place. Once the glue has dried fit the rear panel in place.

6. I made the front piece in 2 panels:
    ● Front panel holding windscreen and wipers Chamfer off both top and bottom. Drill holes to take the wipers. Now round off the ends to fit flush with the sides.
    ● Radiator and bumper panel
This panel is rebated to take the radiator. Using a tenon saw cut down either side and with a sharp chisel remove the wood from the middle. Work the chisel from both sides of the panel. With the recess cut out, measure up a piece of aluminium mesh (as used for repairing car wings) and fit it into the rebate. The mesh is held in place by the three radiator grille bars. A contrasting timber is used for the bars and the headlamps. The ends of the panel are rounded to fit flush with the sides. Both panels are now glued on to the front of the coach.

7. Shape up the dashboard and steering wheel and glue into the coach.

8. The seats are now cut. The easiest and quickest method is to shape up one long length of wood for the seat and one piece for the backs. Cut them to length and glue all the backs on to the seats.

A visit to a dress-making shop will furnish you with some felt – the colour scheme is up to you – I used green for the floor and red for the seats. Wood glue is excellent for sticking the felt onto the wood seats.

9. Perspex is now cut and glued on to the side panels and the back window fitted.

10. The seats are now glued to the floor. Felt is cut and fitted around the seats.

11. The kitchen unit is now made. I made the sink itself by drilling a large diameter hole and the central tap unit is made from a shaped off cut and a small bent piece of aluminium rod. This unit is now glued into the coach.

12. The windscreen is now glued in place. The windscreen wipers are bent from wire and the blades made from pieces of plastic sheet. These look good if they are painted black.

13. The roof is made in one long section. Chamfer off the sides with a plane. Now cut the front roof section off and plane an angle on to the end.

The roof now fits on to the tops of the window

pillars, and when you have a good fit to the front roof section glue the roof in place. The roof hatches are detailed in contrasting timber and the raised portion on the back of the roof is the air conditioning unit.

14. Strips of Brazilian mahogany are used along the coach sides.

15. It is best to apply the varnish before fitting the wheels.

Volvo Luxury Coach Cutting List

Front Panel	1 off 178 × 38 × 16mm (7 × 1½ × ⅝in) timber
Radiator and Bumper Panel	1 off 178 × 51 × 20mm (7 × 2 × ¾in) timber
Driver & Courier Seat	2 off 70 × 38 × 12mm (2¾ × 1½ × ½in) timber
	2 off 38 × 35 × 22mm (1½ × 1⅜ × ⅞in) timber
Passenger Seat	11 off 54 × 44 × 20mm (2⅛ × 1¾ × ¾in) timber
	11 off 54 × 38 × 8mm (2⅛ × 1½ × 5/16in) timber
Lamps	Make from 89 × 9 × 3mm (3½ × ⅜ × ⅛in) timber
Kitchen Unit	1 off 95 × 32 × 25mm (3¾ × 1¼ × 1in) timber
	1 off 95 × 38 × 8mm (3¾ × 1½ × 5/16in) timber
	1 off 76 × 32 × 16mm (3 × 1¼ × ⅝in) timber
	1 off 32 × 8 × 6mm (1¼ × 5/16 × ¼in) timber
Dashboard	1 off 140 × 33 × 8mm (5½ × 1 5/16 × 5/16in) timber
	1 off 28mm (1⅛in) × 5mm (3/16in) diam dowel
	1 off 6mm (¼in) × 35mm (1⅜in) diam dowel
Chassis	1 off 635 × 178 × 20mm (25 × 7 × ¾in) timber
	2 off 212 × 16 × 6mm (8¾ × ⅝ × ¼in) timber
Roof	1 off 559 × 184 × 20mm (22 × 7¼ × ¾in) timber
	1 off 184 × 92 × 20mm (7¼ × 3⅝ × ¾in) timber
	2 off 102 × 76 × 3mm (4 × 3 × ⅛in) timber
	1 off 203 × 152 × 20mm (8 × 6 × ¾in) timber
	2 off 203 × 6 × 3mm (8 × ¼ × ⅛in) timber
Rear Panel	1 off 200 × 178 × 20mm (7⅞ × 7 × ¾in) timber
Side Panel	2 off 635 × 194 × 20mm (25 × 7⅝ × ¾in) timber
	2 off 76 × 12 × 6mm (3 × ½ × ¼in) timber
	Make from 1400 × 16 × 6mm (55 × ⅝ × ¼in) timber
Floor	1 off 140 × 89 × 20mm (5½ × 3½ × ¾in) timber
	1 off 140 × 114 × 20mm (5½ × 4½ × ¾in) timber
	1 off 502 × 140 × 20mm (19¾ × 5½ × ¾in) timber
Ancillaries	6 off 102mm (4in) diam road wheels
	2 off 191mm (7½in) × 6mm (¼in) diam steel axles
	4 off 6mm (¼in) spring dome caps
	1 off 76mm (3in) × 35mm (1⅜in) expanded mesh
	2 off 127mm (5in) × 3mm (⅛in) diam soft wire – wiper arms and tap
	2 off 57 × 6 × 1.5mm (2¼ × ¼ × 1/16in) hard plastic
wiper blades	
	4 off 3mm (⅛in) × 6mm (¼in) 1/diam spacer
	2 off 159 × 92 × 1.5mm (6¼ × 3⅝ × 1/16in) clear plastic door panels
	2 off 527 × 111 × 1.5mm (20¾ × 4⅜ × 1/16in) clear plastic side windows
	1 off 137 × 111 × 1.5mm (5⅜ × 4⅜ × 1/16in) clear plastic rear window
	1 off 159 × 114 × 1.5mm (6¼ × 4½ × 1/16in) clear plastic windscreen

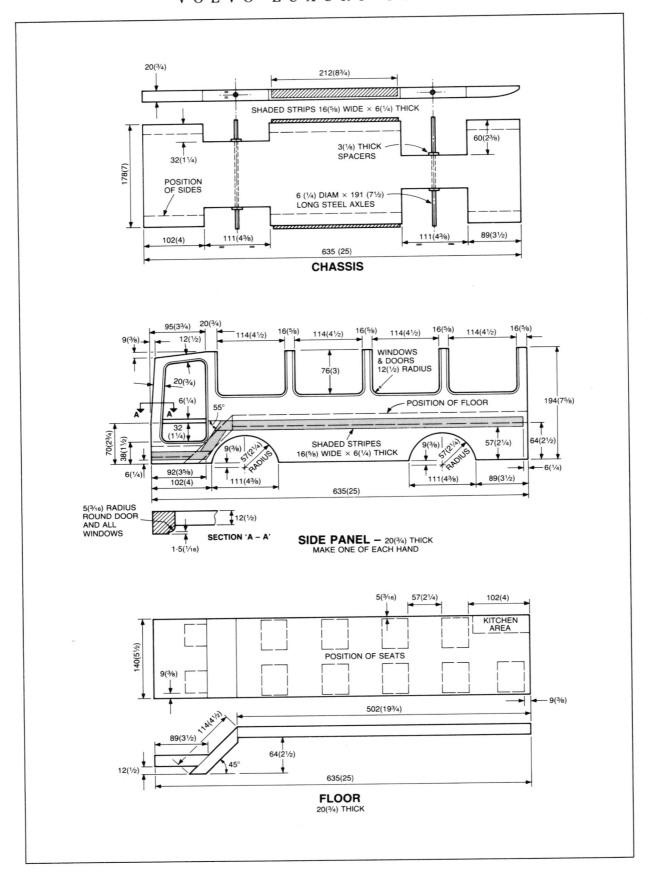

CHASSIS

SIDE PANEL — 20(¾) THICK
MAKE ONE OF EACH HAND

SECTION 'A – A'

FLOOR
20(¾) THICK

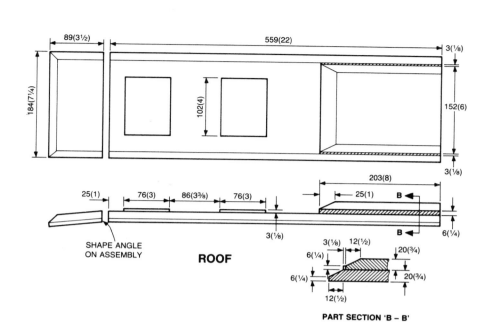

ROOF

PART SECTION 'B – B'

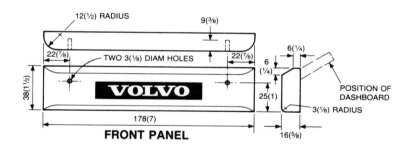

FRONT PANEL

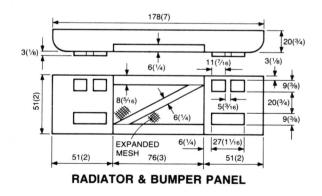

RADIATOR & BUMPER PANEL

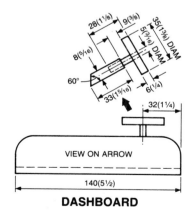

VIEW ON ARROW

DASHBOARD

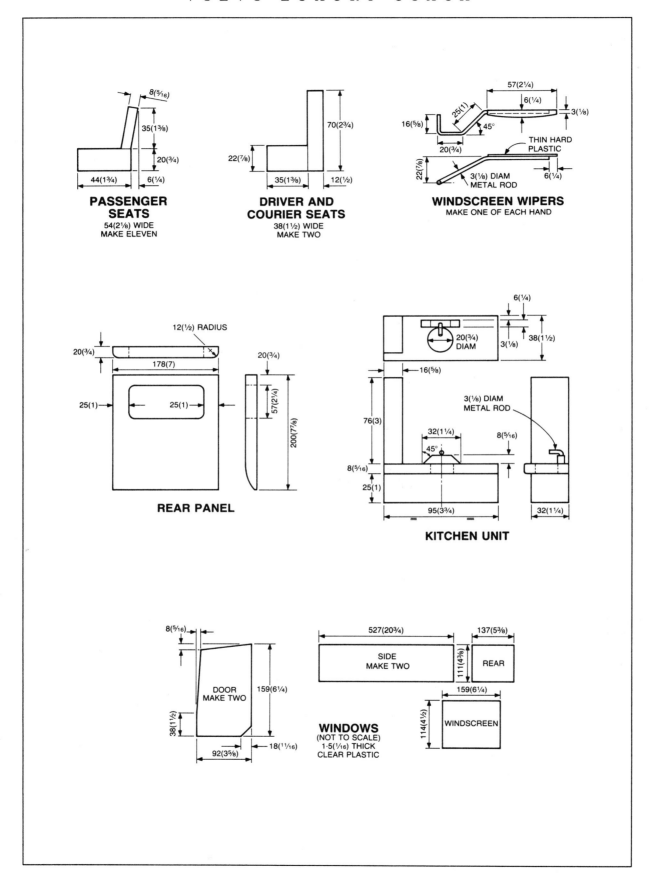

PASSENGER SEATS
54(2⅛) WIDE
MAKE ELEVEN

DRIVER AND COURIER SEATS
38(1½) WIDE
MAKE TWO

WINDSCREEN WIPERS
MAKE ONE OF EACH HAND

THIN HARD PLASTIC
3(⅛) DIAM METAL ROD

REAR PANEL
12(½) RADIUS

KITCHEN UNIT
3(⅛) DIAM METAL ROD

DOOR
MAKE TWO

SIDE
MAKE TWO

REAR

WINDSCREEN

WINDOWS
(NOT TO SCALE)
1·5(1/16) THICK
CLEAR PLASTIC

BARREL ORGAN

(See colour plate 8)

The unique sound of the barrel organ immediately transports one to the streets of Victorian England where these musical machines were common. The large machines had a variety of tunes which the 'musician' could select by turning a lever. I can only assume that there were many 'musical mechanics' engaged in making rollers that played the 'pop tunes' of the day. The mechanism used only plays one tune, but cranking the handle to the correct revolutions per minute gives quite a different 'interpretation' on this tune! The inside of the organ houses the mechanism which is 'boxed in' allowing a small compartment at the other side for small precious objects etc.

TIMBER

The timber used is Brazilian Mahogany and beech, although any timber or plywood will do.

TO MAKE

1.   Make a start by cutting the sides and ends. It is a good idea to get the mechanism at an early stage of construction, ideally before you start, (please see *useful addresses* on page 00).

One side has a hole drilled to take the shaft which is attached to a cranking handle on the outside. It is necessary to counterbore the hole on the inside to allow a sufficient length of shaft to go through the side for attaching the handle and the small securing nut on the outside. To prevent the handle scraping the side, a thin piece of plastic tube is cut and fitted between side and handle.

2.   The body is made by simply gluing the pieces of wood together, (use Evo-stick resin wood glue or similar) there are no complicated joints. After gluing together the sides and ends, the bottom is glued in place.

For these gluing operations light weight clamps are very useful, but I find that masking tape is strong and will hold the pieces together very efficiently while the glue cures (dries).

3.   Now the body is made, the internal divisions can be fitted. Fit the musical box movement to the movement mounting block (screw holes are provided in the mechanism for this) which is in turn glued to the partition wall. It is essential to line up the shaft with the counterbored hole and

accurately 'place' the partition wall at this stage of construction. The partition wall is glued in place. The movement compartment cover is made to be a 'tight fit' and not glued in place, as the movement underneath occasionally requires a spot of oil.

4.   The lid is now 'shaped up' and two thin strips of wood glued to the underside. These two strips need to be carefully positioned as they hold the lid in place and locate the inside edges of the organ body.

5.   Monkeys always cause problems and my attempts to cut and shape this beast caused me great problems — as you can see! For those who, like myself, find cutting and shaping any animal difficult a little grid is given to get you started!

6.   The side frames are cut from beech. Make a pair and before shaping begins, drill the axle hole. Using a coping saw, shape the sides and with a spokeshave or glasspaper remove the saw marks.

The axle is a wooden dowel rod which should now be fitted between the side frames. With the axle in place glue the side frames to the body.

7.   The side frames are strengthened by cross pieces which are glued at the back and front of the organ body. The back legs are cut, shaped and glued to the side frames. A single front leg support is glued on to the body assembly. The front leg stops the organ over-balancing.

8.   Plastic wooden replica wheels are now fitted on to the axle. The wheels are secured by two wooden wheel retainers.

Mark out with a compass two circular discs on a small blank piece of wood. Drill the axle hole in the middle and very carefully cut round the edges. The wheel retainer should now be fitted by gluing it on to the axle.

9.   A nice finishing touch is to line the interior with red or green felt. The wood is finished with Satin Varnish (Evode varnish is non-toxic). I find the best results are obtained by using a cloth, not a brush. 'Cloth on' a small quantity of varnish, allow it to dry, rub down with a very fine glass paper and repeat the operation three times, finishing off with wax polish.

Barrel Organ Cutting List

Carriage Side Frame	2 off 288 × 48 × 8mm (12 × 2 × 5/16in) timber
Cross Members	2 off 95 × 12 × 8mm (3¾ × ½ × 5/16in) timber
Front Support	1 off 57 × 11 × 8mm (2¼ × 7/16 × 5/16in) timber
Rear Legs	2 off 83 × 16 × 8mm (3¼ × 5/8 × 5/16in) timber
Axle	1 off 152mm (6in) × 6mm (¼in) diam dowel
Wheel Retainer	2 off 6mm (¼in) × 11mm (7/16in) diam dowel
Organ Body Side	2 off 171 × 117 × 9mm (6¾ × 45/8 × 3/8in) timber
Organ Body Front and Rear	2 off 111 × 60 × 6mm (43/8 × 23/8 × ¼in) timber
Organ Body Floor	1 off 171 × 60 × 6mm (6¾ × 23/8 × ¼in) timber
Organ Body Lid	1 off 191 × 89 × 9mm (7½ × 3½ × 3/8in) timber
	2 off 159 × 9 × 3mm (6¼ × 3/8 × 1/8in) timber
Keyboard	1 off 171 × 22 × 9mm (6¾ × 7/8 × 3/8in) timber
Movement Compartment Partition	1 off 98 × 60 × 3mm (37/8 × 23/8 × 1/8in) timber
Movement Compartment Cover	1 off 60 × 54 × 5mm (23/8 × 21/8 × 3/16in) timber
Movement Mounting Block	1 off 57 × 36 × 22mm (2¼ × 17/16 × 7/8in) timber
Monkey	1 off 96 × 96 × 8mm (4 × 4 × 5/16in) timber
Ancillaries	1 off Musical Movement
	2 off 79mm (31/8in) diam cart wheels

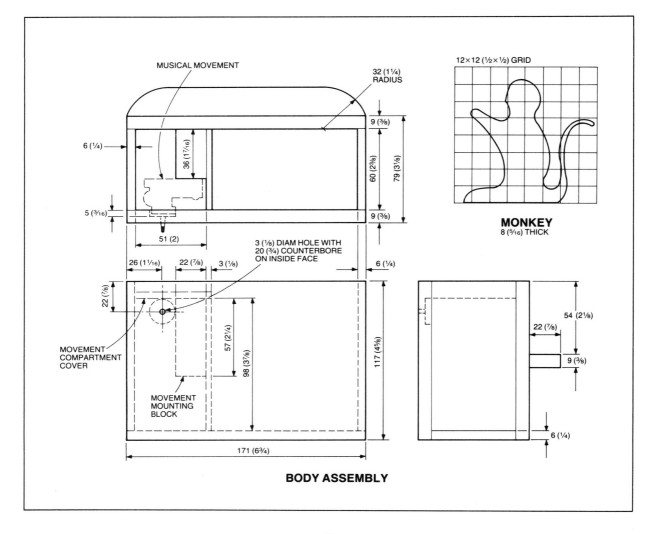

MUSICAL MOVEMENT

32 (1¼) RADIUS

12×12 (½×½) GRID

MONKEY
8 (5/16) THICK

MOVEMENT COMPARTMENT COVER

3 (1/8) DIAM HOLE WITH 20 (¾) COUNTERBORE ON INSIDE FACE

MOVEMENT MOUNTING BLOCK

BODY ASSEMBLY

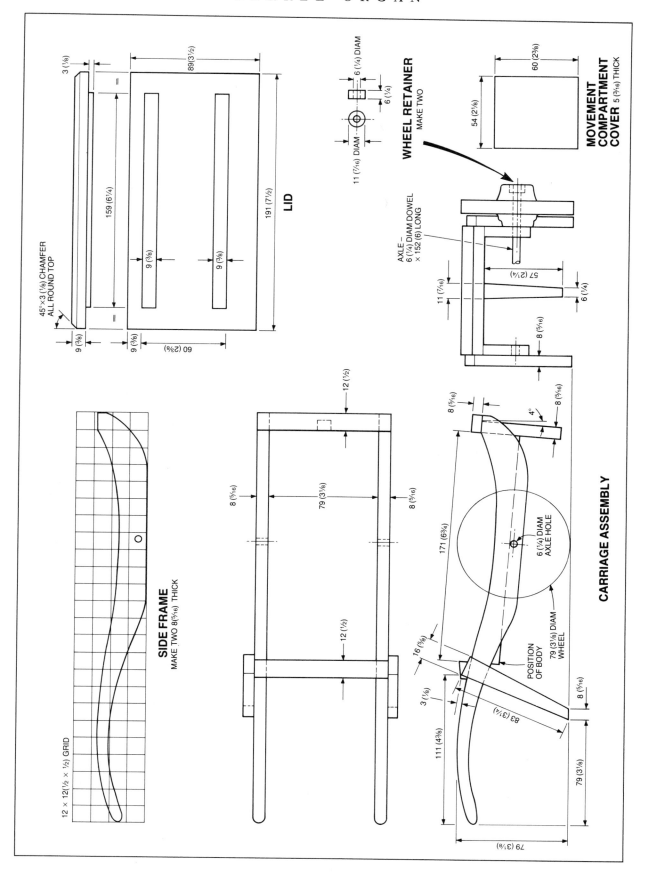

LID

3 (⅛)

89 (3½)

159 (6¼)

191 (7½)

9 (⅜)

9 (⅜)

9 (⅜)

9 (⅜)

9 (⅜)

60 (2⅜)

45° × 3 (⅛) CHAMFER
ALL ROUND TOP

WHEEL RETAINER
MAKE TWO

6 (¼) DIAM

6 (¼)

11 (⁷⁄₁₆) DIAM

MOVEMENT
COMPARTMENT
COVER 5 (³⁄₁₆) THICK

60 (2⅜)

54 (2⅛)

AXLE –
6 (¼) DIAM DOWEL
× 152 (6) LONG

57 (2¼)

11 (⁷⁄₁₆)

8 (⁵⁄₁₆)

6 (¼)

8 (⁵⁄₁₆)

8 (⁵⁄₁₆)

4°

CARRIAGE ASSEMBLY

SIDE FRAME
MAKE TWO 8 (⁵⁄₁₆) THICK

12 × 12 (½ × ½) GRID

12 (½)

8 (⁵⁄₁₆)

79 (3⅛)

8 (⁵⁄₁₆)

12 (½)

171 (6¾)

6 (¼) DIAM
AXLE HOLE

79 (3⅛) DIAM
WHEEL

POSITION
OF BODY

16 (⅝)

3 (⅛)

83 (3¼)

111 (4⅜)

8 (⁵⁄₁₆)

79 (3⅛)

79 (3⅛)

M A N ARTICULATED LORRY AND TRAILER
Truck of the Year 1987

(See colour plate 9)

For those of you who keep an eye on the trucking world, you will know that 'Truck of the Year' is a very prestigious award and much sought after by all the European truck makers. Since this accolade has been awarded, MAN has won the coveted prize three times. This year it was the MAN F90 that won the honour for this Bavarian trucking company.

MAN has a special place in the history of transport for it was to this company that Dr Diesel looked for support and factory facilities when he was pioneering the diesel engine.

This is not a good project for the beginner. It is not really a toy, rather a model of the F90 and requires not only wood-working skills but the ability to bend metal to form springs, and a soldering iron.

TIMBER
The lorry is made with a beech chassis, Brazilian mahogany superstructure headlamps, side lights detailed in ash.

TO MAKE
1. Make a start by studying the chassis assembly drawing. The two chassis members are basically held together by spacers – rear, middle and front. The chassis is secured at the front by two stub mortice and tenon joints that go into the front bumper. This is the basis of the chassis and it's vital to get this right before any of the other work is done.

   The chassis on the real truck bends to a slimmer profile at the back, and to achieve this I have added extra side pieces to the front of the chassis. To give strength at the back, and allow a good anchorage for the trailer hitch (the 5 wheel) I have added 2 extra lengths of beech on the inside edge. Before any marking or cutting can begin it's necessary to glue these extra pieces of wood on to the main chassis members. Once this is done, tape the two chassis sections together and mark out the position of the front axle, the stub mortices at the front, and pencil in all the other fixture positions. It's so much easier to pencil in chassis details at this stage than attempt to do it later.

2. Cut to length the bumper and chop the mortice holes. Shape up and cut the 3 chassis spacers.

Don't glue anything together at this early stage.

3. A fully steerable front axle is essential. Cut out the front axle beam. The 'slots' that take the steering blocks are slightly chamfered on their inside edges to allow the steering blocks to pivot in the axle beam. The steering blocks are designed so that the stub axle holding the front wheel is set forward of the pivot pin. This arrangement works well and prevents the necessity to get involved in any complicated 'king pins'. The stub axle holes that take the front wheels need to be drilled very accurately. Mount the stub axles in the front axle beam, taping them in position and drill the pivot pin hole. In this way you can ensure accuracy. Cut to shape the front axle bearing plate and the steering tie bar.

   Before further assembly make sure that the steering blocks swivel smoothly in the axle beam. Once this is achieved the pivot pins can be driven in. These pins do not need to be fitted with spring clips but are sufficiently tight to 'stay put' in the axle beam. The steering tie bar however is made of much thinner material and should be secured by spring clips.

4. The rear springing on the F90 possesses massive strength so it is necessary to make twin rear springs. The material used is nickel silver spring steel. This material does not rust and is easily worked with round nosed pliers, its only drawback is the expense.

   After cutting all the leaves to length they are soldered together. Now drill the hole for the retaining screw that goes into the back axle. The springs are held to the chassis sides by screws that have cup washers fitted.

5. The rear axle is now cut to length and a hole bored to take the steel axle rod. To prevent any movement of the axle a system of bracing has been designed by MAN. This acts as an 'anti-tramping' bar. Drill the back axle to take 2 dowel rods, and corresponding holes in the chassis. A strong piece of brass wire is now bent and fitted into these dowel rods. The whole unit looks very workmanlike. Before assembling the unit bore a hole to take the prop shaft assembly.

6. Cut and shape the engine block. A fan is fitted

to the front. At the rear of the block a hole is bored to take the prop shaft.

7.   Work on the front bumper and cut the recesses for the headlights. A feature of the truck is the continental curve of the cab front. This curvature is reflected in the bumper. It makes the finished truck look very handsome, but involves a great deal of work at the shaping stage.

Beneath the bumper a spoiler is fitted. The bumper also carries 2 further spot lamps. A great deal of effort has to go into the shaping of these parts.

On top of the bumper it is necessary to fit a mounting strip to take the cab unit. The hinges that take the cab are fitted here. The mounting strip allows the cab to be tilted without fouling the bumper unit. This strip is screwed on to the chassis as it holds the whole cab unit.

8.   Work can now begin on the rear mudguards. These were cut from the solid timber using a bandsaw. I suggest a visit to the local school or a technical college if you do not possess a bandsaw, approached in the right way I am sure they will help.

Cut the centre of the block out first which will allow you to hold it in the vice to remove all the saw marks. Use a fairly large piece of dowel rod wrapped in glasspaper and work carefully around the concave surface. Now cut around the outside edge of the mudguard and carefully glasspaper the surface.

Chamfer off the edges and glue small mounting blocks on to the mudguard. You will find it easier to fit the steel rods to the blocks first as this will help you align things. Shaping mudguards is a time consuming business, but well worth the effort.

9.   Cut and shape the fifth wheel (trailer hitch) air cylinders (dowel rod), battery box, fuel tank and the spare wheel mounting block.

10.   The catwalk is made from 2 strips of wood that are covered with aluminium mesh. The metal ladder is soldered together from pieces of brass wire.

11.   The rear section of the front mudguards is now cut and shaped. Holes are drilled to take the steel or aluminium rods that attach it to the truck chassis.

12.   The cab side front and rear panels are the next job to tackle. Very careful marking out is essential. Rebates are cut on the back and front panels before any other operations. Now cut the windows out. Besides the removal of all saw cuts from window edges I also put a chamfer on here. This chamfer or rounding off of the sharp edge changes the whole appearance of the truck and

makes it look far more stream-lined. The cab of the F90 has beautiful lines and this small detail will enhance it.

The cab front panel has a gentle radius which runs from both sides to the side of the radiator grille. Careful work with a spokeshave is essential to get this line.

The radiator grille is the hall-mark of this machine. The grille bars (9) are glued on to the grille. This is painstaking work and requires a great deal of patience. The radiator grille is then glued on to the cab front panel. The cab is now glued together.

13.   Cab fittings are now made and installed. The steering wheel is made and fitted into the dash board. The luxurious 'arm chairs' are cut out and covered in brown felt. The gear lever and centre console are left uncovered and look very luxurious when polished. The two bunk beds are fitted at the back, and the floor and back panel including the bunks are covered in felt. The windscreen is curved but to achieve this the perspex needs to be longer than the width of the cab. Holes are now drilled into the perspex to take chrome plated round head screws. Fix one side of the windscreen first, then bend the screen and fix it at the other end (more screws). By this method the screen will bow outwards. Now cut a separate piece of wood to the curvature of the screen and glue this on to the front panel. Drill three holes through the perspex for the windscreen wipers. The wipers are made from pieces of bent brass wire with small pieces of plastic glued to them.

14.   Around the cab runs a banding of timber. Once this has been planed you will need a gas kettle to steam it to shape – electric kettles turn themselves off as soon as the water boils so it's a case of allowing the old kettle to boil away, generating a constant flow of steam. If you have never undertaken this sort of work before it's not as difficult or impossible as it sounds, but take care to avoid burning yourself on the steam. Steam is directed on to the piece of wood you wish to bend and after about 5 minutes you will be able to start bending it. It's a combination of heat and water vapour that makes the wood supple – and it's amazing just how easily the timber bends – go too fast and it will crack and you will have to start from the beginning. Once you have achieved the desired curvature, glue the strip on to the cab.

15.   The cab steps are now made and fitted. It's worth cutting out all the parts and assembling them 'dry' (without glue). The reason for this is that when the cab is closed the mudguard on the underside of the cab needs to line up flush with the mudguard attached to the steps. It's so easy to make adjustments before glue is used but very difficult afterwards.

To give the steps extra support it is advisable to glue a small block on to the back of the bumper and step support. The cab steps are covered with aluminium mesh and held in place by epoxy resin glue. The two mudguards at the back of the cab are now fitted. The aluminium rod that holds them to the chassis can be slightly bent if they don't quite line up with the mudguard fixed onto the bottom of the cab.

16. The cab roof is now cut and once again you will need to use a bandsaw to shape the roof spoiler. Make sure that all saw cuts are removed, otherwise when you come to varnish they will show up clearly.

NOTES ON FINAL ASSEMBLY

When building a model it is necessary only to assemble some of the major parts, but there are stages like building the cab and mudguards when it's important to get some things glued together in order to get the datum lines fixed for the next task. The chassis must be glued at an early stage but try to avoid adding all the accessories until nearly finished. I found it necessary to varnish each piece individually and finish them off before gluing or fixing to the chassis or cab.

It's really a case of adopting a scheme of working which in the long run makes things far easier.

I never apply varnish with a brush but use a lint free cloth. It is best to use glasspaper between each application and finish off with wax polish.

Do make sure that pieces individually varnished are not 'contaminated' with varnish where they have to be attached to the chassis or cab – they just won't stick if that happens. Mark the glue areas with a pencil cross just to remind yourself.

THE TRAILER

1. First mark out all the joints on the two parallel chassis members. Now make the eight chassis spacer pieces. Put all the pieces together and mark them all out together – this ensures accuracy. Cut the stub mortices and tenons and fit the chassis together.

2. Cut a pair of rear axle frames and drill holes to take the steel axle rods and cut rebates onto the top edges. The rear mudguards are cut from the solid. It's easier to remove the wood waste from the inside, glasspaper away the saw marks and then work on the outside edge.

3. The frame holding the safety bars on the outside doubles as a useful mounting position for the spare wheels.

4. A jockey wheel frame is essential when the trailer is parked without the lorry.

5. Onto the trailer chassis is mounted a piece of plywood. This is secured by screws that pass from beneath through the eight spacers.

6. The trailer sides can be left just plain or if you have a thin plough plane cutter you can plough grooves along the full length of the sides to simulate planking. Once this is completed reinforcement strips of wood are glued along the length of the sides, this looks very effective.

7. Many articulated trailers are of the canvas covered type. If you wish to convert the trailer to one of these then drill (very very carefully) holes along the trailer sides. Using a thick braided plastic fuel pipe (this can be found in a motor shop) threaded on to aluminium tube, bend the supports to shape.

8. Now comes the job of measuring up the top, getting some assistance from someone who has skills with a sewing machine.

M A N Articulated Lorry and Trailer Cutting List

Chassis Main Member	2 off 533 × 38 × 11mm (21 × 1½ × 7/16in) timber
Chassis Side Member	2 off 305 × 38 × 11mm (12 × 1½ × 7/16in) timber
Chassis Rear Reinforcing	2 off 178 × 38 × 11mm (7 × 1½ × 7/16in) timber
Front Spacer	1 off 73 × 38 × 12mm (2⅞ × 1½ × ½in) timber
Middle Spacer	1 off 81 × 32 × 12mm (3³/₁₆ × 1¼ × ½in) timber
Rear Spacer	1 off 73 × 22 × 20mm (2⅞ × ⅞ × ¾in) timber
Cab Mounting Strip	1 off 203 × 20 × 9mm (8 × ¾ × ⅜in) timber
Bumper	1 off 228 × 46 × 25mm (9 × 1³/₁₆ × 1in) timber
Side, Headlights and Spotlamps	Make from 178 × 14 × 1.5mm (7 × 9/16 × 1/16in) timber
Spoiler	1 off 228 × 12 × 9mm (9 × ½ × ⅜in) timber
Step Assembly	2 off 83 × 76 × 8mm (3¼ × 3 × 5/16in) timber
	2 off 44 × 22 × 12mm (1¾ × ⅞ × ½in) timber
	2 off 89 × 21 × 11mm (3½ × 13/16 × 7/16in) timber
	Make from 203 × 21 × 5mm (8 × 13/16 × 3/16in) timber

M A N Articulated Lorry and Trailer Cutting List *continued*

Battery Box	1 off 83 × 32 × 6mm (3¼ × 1¼ × ¼in) timber
	1 off 70 × 38 × 22mm (2¾ × 1½ × ⅞in) timber
Air Cylinders	1 off 89 × 38 × 6mm (3½ × 1½ × ¼in) timber
	2 off 57mm (2¼in) × 22mm (⅞in) diam dowel
	1 off 57mm (2¼in) × 35mm (1⅜in) diam dowel
Fuel Tank	1 off 98 × 60 × 54mm (3⅞ × 2⅜ × 2⅛in) timber
Fuel Tank Supports	2 off 40mm (1⁹⁄₁₆in) × 6mm (¼in) diam dowel
Fuel Tank Filler Cap	1 off 20mm (¾in) × 6mm (¼in) diam dowel
	1 off 6mm (¼in) × 12mm (½in) diam dowel
Walkway	2 off 159 × 12 × 6mm (6¼ × ½ × ¼in) timber
Fifth Wheel	1 off 102 × 89 × 6mm (4 × 3½ × ¼in) timber
	1 off 95 × 64 × 12mm (3¾ × 2½ × ½in) timber
Spare Wheel Mounting	1 off 44 × 22 × 22mm (1¾ × ⅞ × ⅞in) timber
Front Mudguard	2 off 89 × 41 × 20mm (3½ × 1⅝ × ¾in) timber
Rear Mudguard	2 off 126 × 75 × 64mm (5 × 3 × 2¼in) timber
	4 off 20 × 12 × 6mm (¾ × ½ × ¼in) timber
	4 off 25 × 12 × 6mm (1 × ½ × ¼in) timber
Engine and Gearbox	1 off 184 × 69 × 41mm (7¼ × 2¾ × 1⅝in)
Fan	1 off 60 × 60 × 6mm (2⅜ × 2⅜ × ¼in) timber
Prop Shaft	1 off 238mm (9in) × 12mm (½in) diam dowel
Front Axle Beam	1 off 152 × 38 × 20mm (6 × 1½ × ¾in) timber
Front Axle Bearing Plate	1 off 152 × 28 × 9mm (6 × 1⅛ × ⅜in) timber
Steering Tie Bar	1 off 152 × 35 × 9mm (6 × 1⅜ × ⅜in) timber
Steering Blocks	2 off 64 × 35 × 16mm (2½ × 1⅜ × ⅝in) timber
Rear Axle	1 off 108 × 35 × 20mm (4¼ × 1⅜ × ¾in) timber
	2 off 47mm (1⅞in) × 9mm (⅜in) diam dowel
	2 off 20mm (¾in) × 9mm (⅜in) diam dowel
Drivers Mirror	1 off 41 × 20 × 6mm (1⅝ × ¾ × ¼in) timber
Passengers Mirror	1 off 28 × 20 × 6mm (1⅛ × ¾ × ¼in) timber
	1 off 25 × 16 × 6mm (1 × ⅝ × ¼in) timber
Cab Rear Panel	1 off 225 × 187 × 12mm (8⅞ × 7⅜ × ½in) timber
	2 off 201 × 38 × 6mm (7⅞ × 1½ × ¼in) timber
	2 off 213 × 22 × 1.5mm (8⅜ × ⅞ × ¹⁄₁₆in) timber
Cab Roof	1 off 225 × 191 × 12mm (8⅞ × 7½ × ½in) timber
	1 off 174 × 146 × 9mm (6⅞ × 5¾ × ⅜in) timber
	1 off 86 × 35 × 12mm (3⅜ × 1⅜ × ½in) timber
	1 off 206 × 64 × 56mm (8⅛ × 2½ × 2¼in) timber
Cab Side	2 off 184 × 175 × 12mm (7¼ × 6⅞ × ½in) timber
	2 off 175 × 22 × 1.5mm (6⅞ × ⅞ × ¹⁄₁₆in) timber
Door Handle	2 off 25 × 6 × 5mm (1 × ¼ × ³⁄₁₆in) timber
Upper Mudguard	2 off 120 × 32 × 14mm (4¹¹⁄₁₆ × 1¼ × ⁹⁄₁₆in) timber
Cab Front Panel	1 off 225 × 92 × 20mm (8⅞ × 3⅝ × ¾in) timber
	1 off 241 × 22 × 1.5mm (9½ × ⅞ × ¹⁄₁₆in) timber
	1 off 201 × 9 × 6mm (7⅞ × ⅜ × ¼in) timber
Radiator Grille	1 off 114 × 54 × 6mm (4½ × 2⅛ × ¼in) timber
	Make from 1362 × 3 × 1.5mm (53¾ × ⅛ × ¹⁄₁₆in) timber
	1 off 10 × 9 × 1.5mm (⁷⁄₁₆ × ⅜ × ¹⁄₁₆in) timber
Cab Floor	1 off 200 × 165 × 12mm (7⅞ × 6½ × ½in) timber
Engine Cover	1 off 60 × 44 × 20mm (2⅜ × 1¾ × ¾in) timber
Gear Lever	1 off 20 × 16 × 9mm (¾ × ⅝ × ⅜in) timber
	1 off 20mm (¾in) × 9mm (⅜in) diam dowel
Seat	2 off 89 × 54 × 51mm (3½ × 2⅛ × 2in) timber
Arm Rest	2 off 47 × 9 × 6mm (1⅞ × ⅜ × ¼in) timber
Dashboard	1 off 197 × 43 × 25mm (7¾ × 1¹¹⁄₁₆ × 1in) timber
Steering Wheel	1 off 6mm (¼in) × 32mm (1¼in) diam dowel
	1 off 41mm (1⅝in) × 6mm (¼in) diam dowel

M A N Articulated Lorry and Trailer Cutting List *continued*

Ancillaries	7 off 102mm (4in) diam road wheels
	2 off 76mm (3in) × 6mm (1/4in) diam steel stub axles
	2 off 6mm (1/4in) × 6mm (1/4in) 1/diam hard plastic spacers
	1 off 222mm (8 3/4in) × 6mm (1/4in) diam steel rear axle
	4 off 6mm (1/4in) spring dome caps
	4 off 51mm (2in) × 3mm (1/8in) diam steel rods front mudguard
	4 off 81mm (3 3/16in) × 3mm (1/8in) diam steel rods rear mudguards
	2 off 38mm (1 1/2in) × 5mm (3/16in) diam steel pivot pins
	2 off 32mm (1 1/4in) × 5mm (3/16in) diam steel pivot pins
	4 off 5mm (3/16in) spring dome caps
	2 off 25mm (1in) brass hinges
	1 off 159mm (6 1/4in) × 47mm (1 7/8in) expanded mesh – walkway
	Make from 381mm (15in) × 1.5mm (1/16) diam soft wire walkway ladder
	1 off 140mm (5 1/2in) × 3mm (1/8in) diam wire rear axle
	Make from 1604 × 16 × 1.5mm (63 1/2 × 5/8 × 1/16in) spring steel
	1 off 203mm (8in) × 21mm (13/16in) wire mesh step covering
	Make from 330mm (13in) × 1.5mm (1/16in) diam soft wire mirror arms
	2 off 102mm (4in) × 1.5mm (1/16in) diam soft wire rear cab hand rails
	1 off 225 × 92 × 1.5mm (8 7/8 × 3 5/8 × 1/16in) clear plastic windscreen
	2 off 121 × 111 × 1.5mm (4 3/4 × 4 3/8 × 1/16in) clear plastic side screens
	Make from 210mm (8 1/4in) × 1.5mm (1/16in) diam soft wire wiper arms
	3 off 47 × 6 × 1.5mm (1 7/8 × 1/4 × 1/16in) stiff black plastic wiper blades
	1 off 12mm (1/2in) screwed hook and eye and short length of cord to limit cab tilting

M.A.N. Trailer Cutting List

Main Chassis Members	2 off 1016 × 35 × 12mm (40 × 1 3/8 × 1/2in) timber
Main Chassis Cross Members	8 off 115 × 35 × 22mm (4 1/2 × 1 3/8 × 7/8in) timber
Rear Cross Bar	1 off 184 × 35 × 6mm (7 1/4 × 1 3/8 × 1/4in) timber
Hitch Pin	1 off 73mm (2 7/8in) × 6mm (1/4in) diam dowel
Spare Wheel Mounting and Safety Frame	2 off 209 × 38 × 9mm (8 1/4 × 1 1/2 × 3/8in) timber
	2 off 388 × 20 × 9mm (15 1/4 × 3/4 × 3/8in) timber
	2 off 388 × 12 × 9mm (15 1/4 × 1/2 × 3/8in) timber
	4 off 44mm (1 3/4in) × 6mm (1/4in) diam dowel
Jockey Wheel Assembly	2 off 140 × 25 × 9mm (5 1/2 × 1 × 3/8in) timber
	1 off 145mm (5 3/4in) × 9mm (3/8in) diam dowel
Rear Axle Support Frame	2 off 391 × 83 × 20mm (15 3/8 × 3 1/4 × 3/4in) timber
	2 off 140 × 35 × 9mm (5 1/2 × 1 3/8 × 3/8in) timber
	1 off 228 × 35 × 6mm (9 × 1 3/8 × 1/4in) timber
Rear Mudguard	2 off 362 × 72 × 35mm (14 1/4 × 2 7/8 × 1 3/8in) timber
Trailer Bed Sides	2 off 1159 × 70 × 20mm (45 5/8 × 2 3/4 × 3/4in) timber
Trailer End Panels	2 off 221 × 70 × 20mm (8 3/4 × 2 3/4 × 3/4in) timber
Trailer Floor	1 off 1159 × 203 × 9mm (45 5/8 × 8 × 3/8in) timber
Side Strips	18 off 70 × 11 × 1.5mm (2 3/4 × 7/16 × 1/16in) timber

Ancillaries

8 off 102mm (4in) diam road wheels
3 off 228mm (9in) × 6mm (¼in) diam steel axles
6 off 6mm (¼in) × 6mm (¼in) ⅟diam plastic spacers
6 off 6mm (¼in) spring dome caps
2 off 25mm (1in) diam jockey wheels
1 off 178mm (7in) × 5mm (³⁄₁₆in) diam steel rod
1 off 127mm (5in) × 5mm (³⁄₁₆in) ⅟diam hard plastic tube
2 off 5mm (³⁄₁₆in) spring dome caps
Make from 3170mm (125in) × 6mm (¼in) diam
    aluminium rod cover support
Make from 2920mm (115in) × 6mm (¼in) ⅟diam braided
    plastic fuel pipe sheath

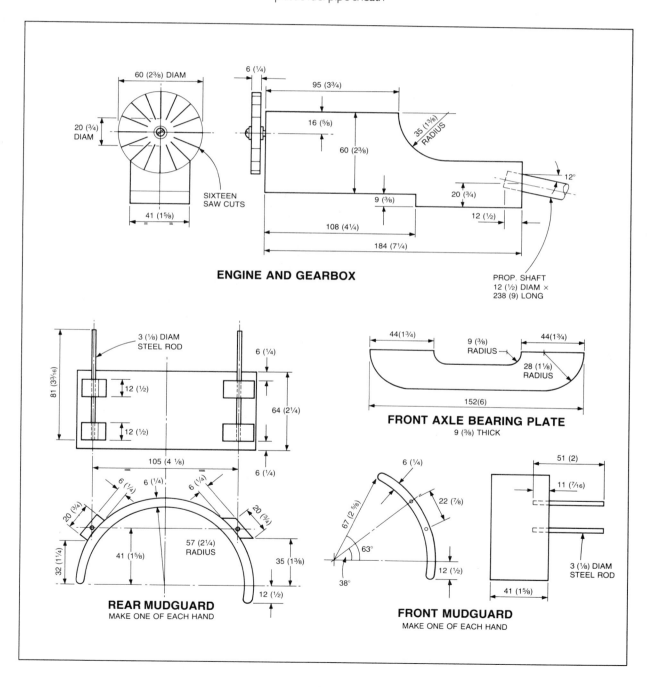

ENGINE AND GEARBOX

PROP. SHAFT
12 (½) DIAM ×
238 (9) LONG

FRONT AXLE BEARING PLATE
9 (³⁄₈) THICK

REAR MUDGUARD
MAKE ONE OF EACH HAND

FRONT MUDGUARD
MAKE ONE OF EACH HAND

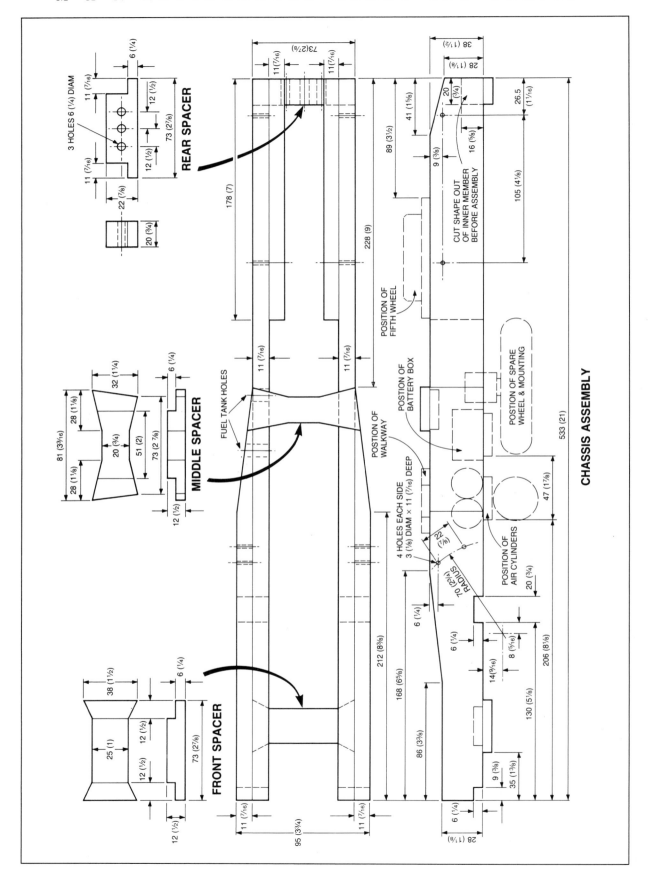

REAR SPACER

3 HOLES 6 (¼) DIAM

MIDDLE SPACER

FUEL TANK HOLES

FRONT SPACER

POSITION OF FIFTH WHEEL

POSTION OF BATTERY BOX

POSTION OF WALKWAY

CUT SHAPE OUT OF INNER MEMBER BEFORE ASSEMBLY

POSTION OF SPARE WHEEL & MOUNTING

POSITION OF AIR CYLINDERS

4 HOLES EACH SIDE 3 (⅛) DIAM × 11 (⁷⁄₁₆) DEEP

70 (2¾) RADIUS

CHASSIS ASSEMBLY

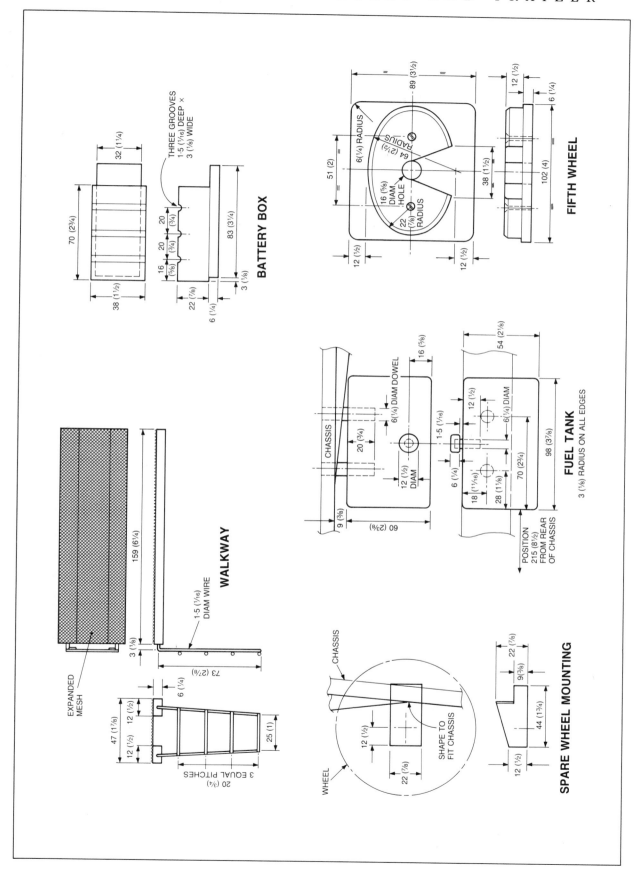

BATTERY BOX

FIFTH WHEEL

FUEL TANK

3 (⅛) RADIUS ON ALL EDGES

WALKWAY

SPARE WHEEL MOUNTING

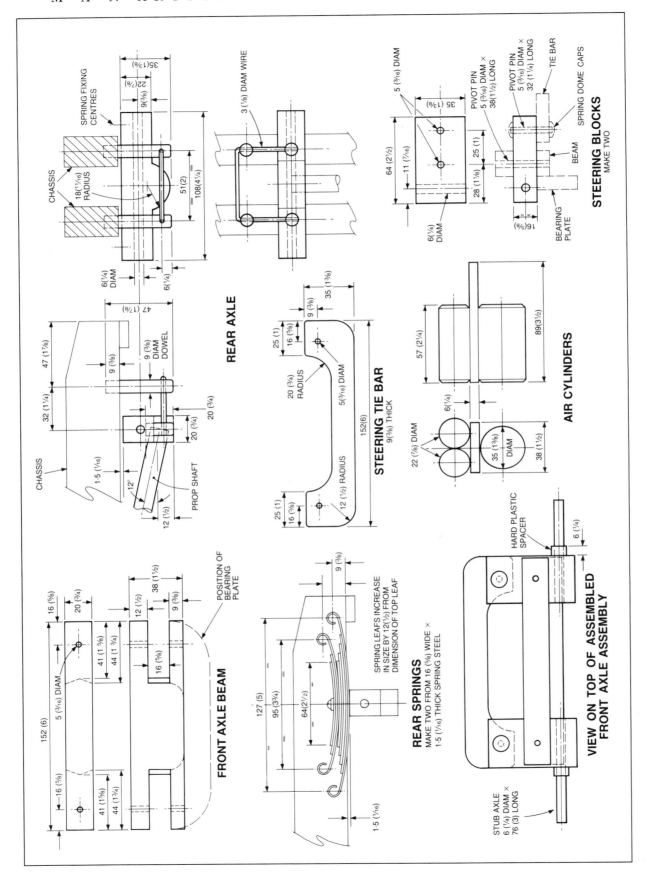

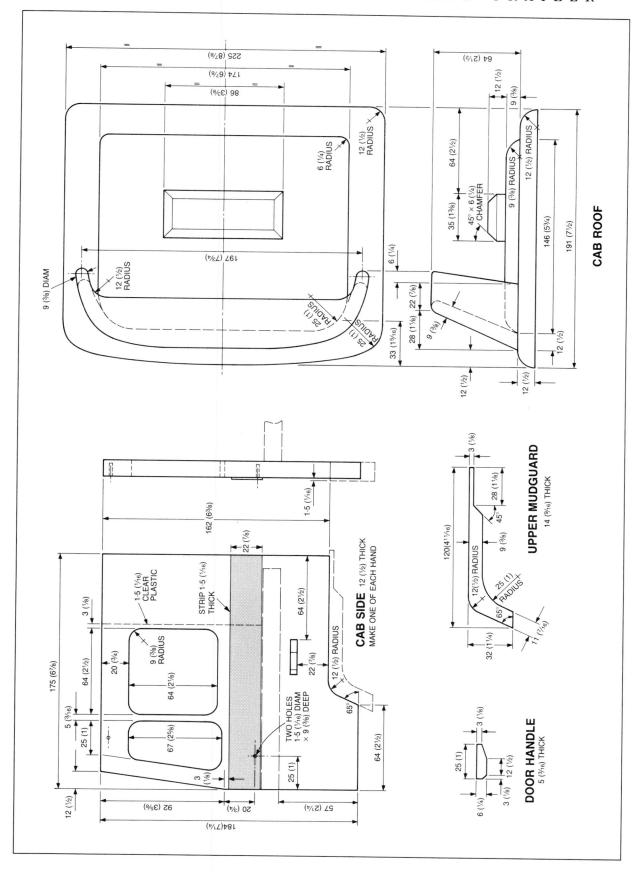

CAB ROOF

CAB SIDE 12 (½) THICK
MAKE ONE OF EACH HAND

UPPER MUDGUARD
14 (⁹⁄₁₆) THICK

DOOR HANDLE
5 (³⁄₁₆) THICK

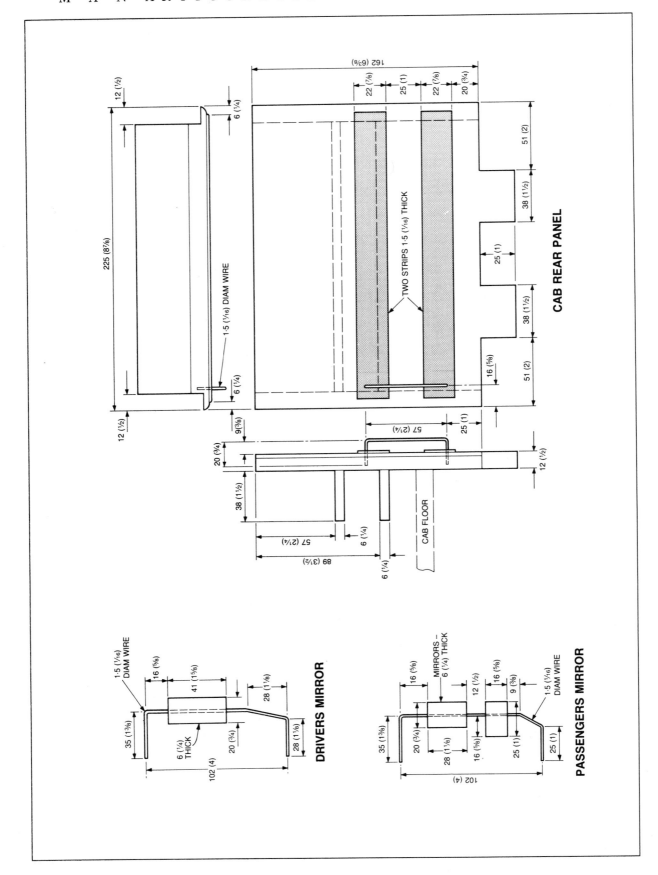

CAB REAR PANEL

DRIVERS MIRROR

PASSENGERS MIRROR

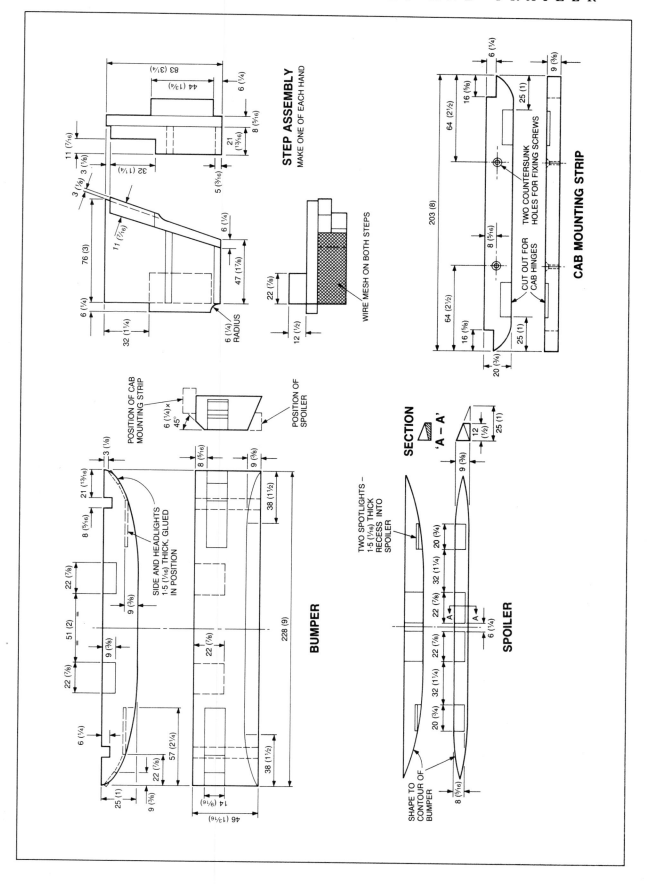

STEP ASSEMBLY
MAKE ONE OF EACH HAND

WIRE MESH ON BOTH STEPS

CAB MOUNTING STRIP

TWO COUNTERSUNK
HOLES FOR FIXING SCREWS

CUT OUT FOR
CAB HINGES

POSITION OF CAB
MOUNTING STRIP

POSITION OF
SPOILER

SIDE AND HEADLIGHTS
1·5 (¹⁄₁₆) THICK, GLUED
IN POSITION

BUMPER

RADIUS

SECTION
'A – A'

TWO SPOTLIGHTS –
1·5 (¹⁄₁₆) THICK
RECESS INTO
SPOILER

SPOILER

SHAPE TO
CONTOUR OF
BUMPER

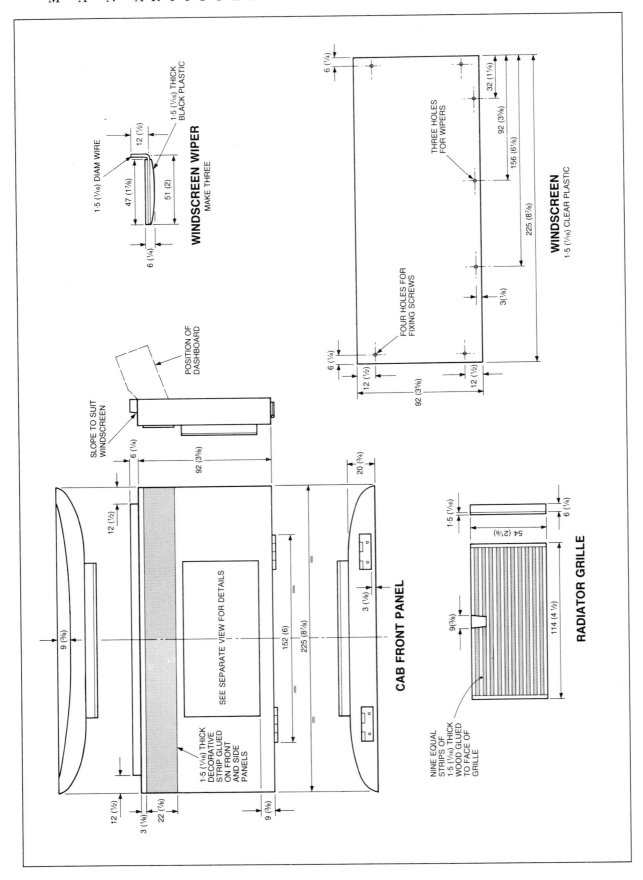

WINDSCREEN WIPER
MAKE THREE

1·5 (¹⁄₁₆) THICK BLACK PLASTIC

1·5 (¹⁄₁₆) DIAM WIRE

12 (½)
47 (1⁷⁄₈)
51 (2)
6 (¼)

WINDSCREEN
1·5 (¹⁄₁₆) CLEAR PLASTIC

THREE HOLES FOR WIPERS
FOUR HOLES FOR FIXING SCREWS

6 (¼)
32 (1¼)
92 (3⁵⁄₈)
156 (6¹⁄₈)
225 (8⁷⁄₈)
3 (¹⁄₈)
12 (½)
92 (3⁵⁄₈)
12 (½)

CAB FRONT PANEL

POSITION OF DASHBOARD
SLOPE TO SUIT WINDSCREEN
SEE SEPARATE VIEW FOR DETAILS

1·5 (¹⁄₁₆) THICK DECORATIVE STRIP GLUED ON FRONT AND SIDE PANELS

9 (³⁄₈)
6 (¼)
92 (3⁵⁄₈)
20 (³⁄₄)
12 (½)
3 (¹⁄₈)
152 (6)
225 (8⁷⁄₈)
12 (½)
3 (¹⁄₈)
22 (⁷⁄₈)
9 (³⁄₈)

RADIATOR GRILLE

NINE EQUAL STRIPS OF 1·5 (¹⁄₁₆) THICK WOOD GLUED TO FACE OF GRILLE

1·5 (¹⁄₁₆)
6 (¼)
54 (2¹⁄₈)
9 (³⁄₈)
114 (4½)

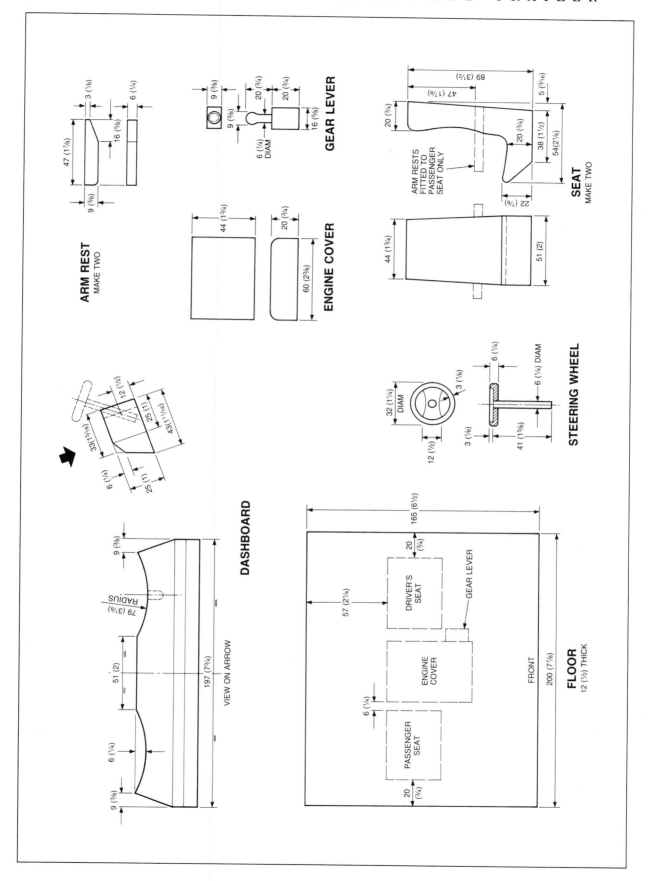

ARM REST
MAKE TWO

GEAR LEVER

ENGINE COVER

SEAT
MAKE TWO

ARM RESTS
FITTED TO
PASSENGER
SEAT ONLY

STEERING WHEEL

DASHBOARD

VIEW ON ARROW

FLOOR
12 (½) THICK

DRIVER'S
SEAT

ENGINE
COVER

PASSENGER
SEAT

GEAR LEVER

FRONT

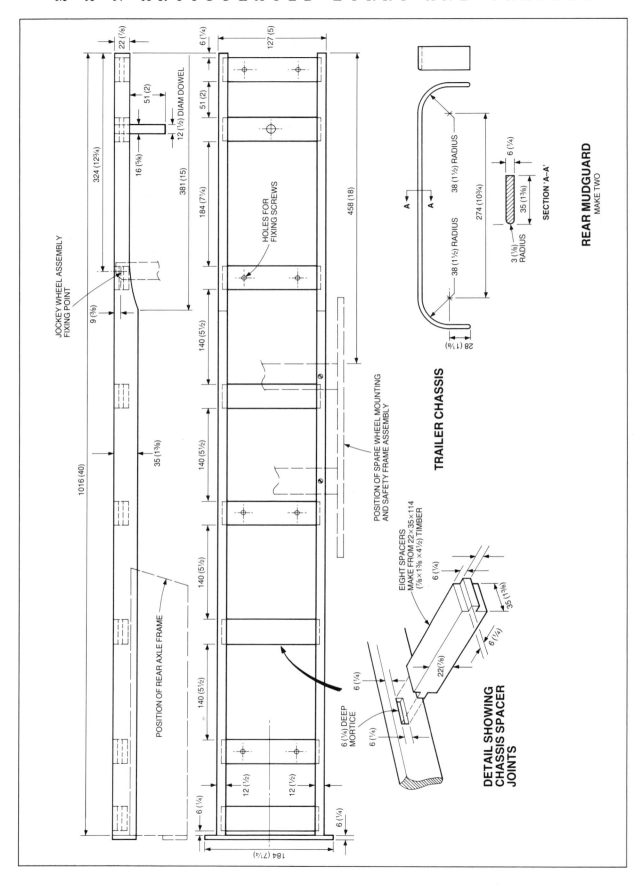

TRAILER CHASSIS

REAR MUDGUARD
MAKE TWO

DETAIL SHOWING CHASSIS SPACER JOINTS

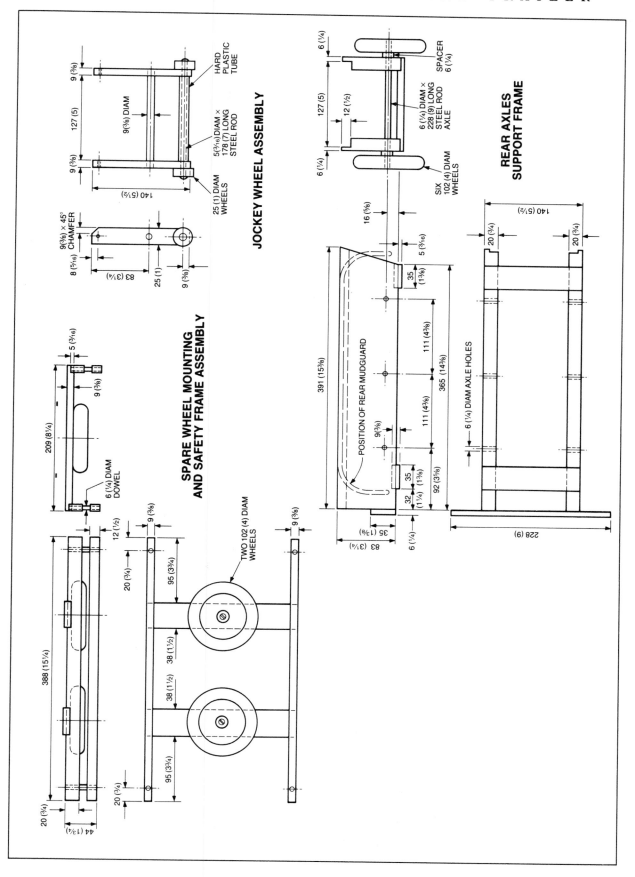

JOCKEY WHEEL ASSEMBLY

REAR AXLES SUPPORT FRAME

SPARE WHEEL MOUNTING AND SAFETY FRAME ASSEMBLY

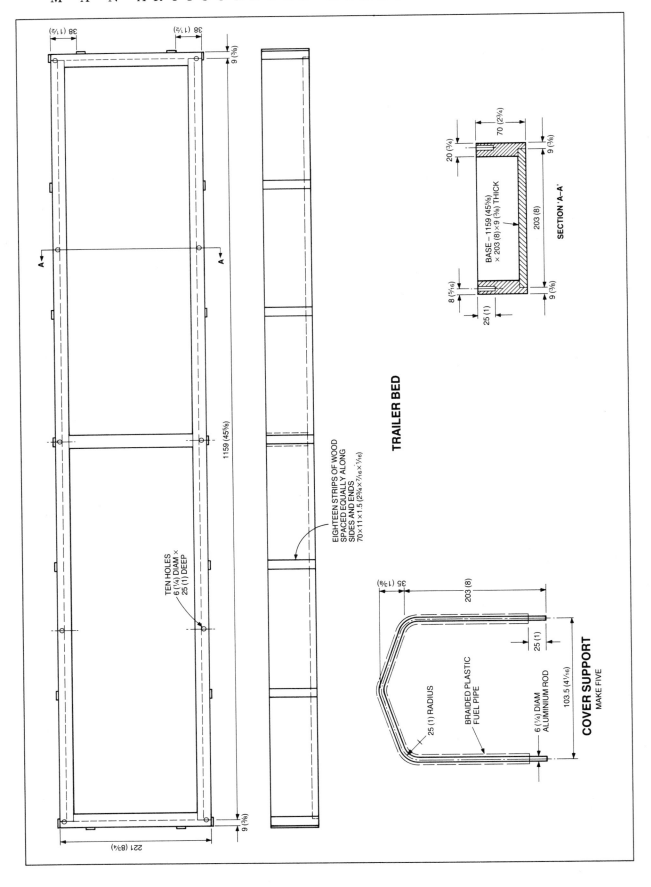

38 (1½)

38 (1½)

9 (⅜)

TEN HOLES
6 (¼) DIAM ×
25 (1) DEEP

1159 (45⅝)

9 (⅜)

221 (8¾)

EIGHTEEN STRIPS OF WOOD
SPACED EQUALLY ALONG
SIDES AND ENDS
70×11×1.5 (2¾×⁷⁄₁₆×¹⁄₁₆)

TRAILER BED

70 (2¾)

20 (¾)

9 (⅜)

BASE – 1159 (45⅝)
× 203 (8) × 9 (⅜) THICK

203 (8)

8 (⁵⁄₁₆)

9 (⅜)

25 (1)

SECTION 'A–A'

35 (1⅜)

203 (8)

25 (1)

25 (1) RADIUS

BRAIDED PLASTIC
FUEL PIPE

6 (¼) DIAM
ALUMINIUM ROD

103.5 (4¹⁄₁₆)

COVER SUPPORT
MAKE FIVE

QUARRY CRANE

(See colour plate 10)

Large trucks are always popular but their use and play value can be greatly enhanced by having a large crane that is capable of loading them up with rock, stone or sand.

This giant crane is immensely strong and can be used to lift all kinds of things, or with the adddition of the hopper can be used to fill the lorry with sand.

The crane can be traversed through 360 degrees and the boom arm is adjustable. When heavy side lifting is required adjustable jacks can be extended from the base and these have provision for working on flat or uneven surfaces. The crane is ideal as a companion for the MAN six wheel truck. The crane is built from stock size Finnish redwood. The inspiration to build the crane came after watching a Ransomes Crane at work on site.

TIMBER
The timber used is Nordic Redwood.

TO MAKE
1. Cut to length the two side members of the crane base, tape them together and drill the holes as shown on the plan.

2. The jacks themselves are made from dowel rods and slide the full width of the base and fit into a drilled hole in the opposite side member when not in use. This provision of holes for the ends of the jacks means that when the jacks are folded they remain in place. Small wooden 'collars' are glued on to the ends of the jacks to prevent the jack being pulled out of the base. The collar has to be fitted a small way down the dowel rod to allow the dowel to go into the pre-drilled 'keeper' hole.

The jack leg itself is made with one end longer than the other. This enables the operator to turn the jack leg round and get extra reach when the surface is uneven. The other dowel rods in the base are for rigidity and keep the base from flexing.

3. Now cut and fit the three pieces of wood that go on the top. The centre one has a hole drilled to take a coach bolt.

4. The crane body has no difficult joints and is held together by the base top and ends. To give strength, the ends, top and bottom are rebated. The easiest method is to select a board that amounts to the total length required and simply rebate the sides. Cut off the top, bottom and ends etc. from the one single length. This method saves time.

Just a note about the rebate joint — it is very useful as it increases the gluing area of a joint and therefore makes it considerably stronger. It also helps when it comes to gluing things together as once the sides are in the rebates, the joint itself keeps the job together. There are two main methods of cutting this joint:

- The traditional way is with a rebate plane but if you don't already have one of these then the second method is worth considering and in the long run less expensive.

- Many woodworkers have a small router. A router cutter for rebating is very useful for many different kinds of jobs. If you don't have a router, I think it's probably the most versatile and useful piece of equipment since the hammer was invented!

5. The crane body sides should be taped together and the various holes drilled as shown on the plan. Drill the hole that takes the coach bolt in the base. Now the top, bottom and front rebated pieces can be glued in place. The back and front pieces surrounding the jib are not glued but screwed into place. Use cup washers under the screw heads. These two panels are necessary for repairs, stringing and re-stringing the crane.

6. The nylon cords that activate the boom and line pass through holes that have to be bored at two different angles, (see drawings on page 00). By drilling the angles indicated and the holes well oversize it will prevent the cables rubbing as they work.

7. Next the jib has to be made. Tape together the two sides and mark the position of the dowel rods, noting that the one at the base is larger in diameter and that the last one at the opposite end is much smaller. Drill all the holes. Now make yourself a small jig so that all the dowel rods are cut off to exactly the same lengths. With a sheet of glasspaper chamfer off the ends of all the dowel rods.

Now separate the two sides, making sure that a pencil mark is placed on both sides so that they can be put back together exactly as they were drilled. On the inside edges lightly countersink all the holes. The reason for all this work is so that when all the dowels are in one side the other ends will line up more easily on the opposite side.

Put a spot of glue on each dowel rod and tap into place. 'Offer up' the other side and, (a bit tricky) get all the dowel rods into the holes. Don't panic and get one end in first, but get all the dowels in the holes the full length of the side. Put the side in the vice and begin to pull the sides together. The even pressure of a vice jaw is so much better than a hammer and a block of wood. Work the jib backwards and forwards in the vice, gently squeezing the sides up all the time. Once the dowel rods are through to the outer edge of the sides you will find the vice tightens and apart from the final planing off and fitting of the screw eyes in the top, the job's done.

8.   Now the pulley wheels that hold the rigging have to be mounted, so carefully follow the plans on page 00. The holes in the upright section are there for decoration, but they look workmanlike, so don't leave them out! When fitting the pulley wheels don't forget to insert the small piece of plastic tube between the two — it acts as a spacer. The axles on which the pulleys run are steel and fitted with spring caps.

9.   Little hands require large levers and handles if they are going to be able to operate things. The two winding discs are carefully marked out and the first task is to drill a hole in the middle to take the winding rod to which the cord is attached. Don't drill this hole right through the handle disc. Now drill on the opposite side to allow a handle to be fitted to the disc.

10.   If a crane is to work satisfactorily then some method must be used to hold either the boom or the line at different positions, and for this the little wooden cogs have to be made. In theory these would be best in plywood, however in practice the ordinary redwood works well and I have never had any 'shearings' of cogs due to the end grain breaking. The secret of making successful cogs is to mark out carefully with a pencil first. While the cog is in 'the square', drill the hole for the winding rod. With a tenon saw start cutting out the cogs — it's not as difficult as it sounds. Wood 'toggles' are now cut and fitted to locate in the cog and in this way the crane's line and boom are infinitely adjustable.

11.   Fit the coach bolt through the base.

12.   The winding rods are now glued into the discs, threaded through the sides, use a little candle wax here, and the cog glued on the other end. When you cut off the excess rod protruding through the cog, leave a small piece 'proud' and you will find that this gives a stronger bonding between

rod and cog. Screw eyes are now fitted to the winding rods as anchorage places for the cord. The eyes should be in line with the holes drilled in the back piece.

13.   The jib is now fitted into the crane body. Once again wherever wood meets wood a little candle wax will be needed. The dowel rod fitted through the sides, holding the bottom of the jib is secured by wooden keeper blocks one on each end. One keeper block is glued in place, the other secured by a screw thus allowing the jib to be removed for servicing.

14.   If you intend to move sand then it's well worth the effort to make a hopper. This is a plywood box construction with the top missing. A large hole is drilled at the bottom and a lever acts as a 'stop' on the sand when the hopper is loading or off loading.

15.   Mount the cab of the crane on to the base. I found it was best done without any washer between the two. The amount of friction that is generated between the two pieces is very useful when winding the handles and prevents the crane body moving. A couple of nuts on the underside will prevent the crane cab working loose when working.

16.   Rigging the crane is not difficult and I chose to use two different coloured cords. This is also quite useful when identifying what each handle is doing and for a small child it is helpful to paint the handle green that raises and lowers the green cord.

Tie the ends of the both cords on to the hooks attached to the winding rods, through the back around the 2 sets of pulleys and through the screw eyes at the end of the jib. The length of line depends entirely how far you want to work away from the crane. I suggest that 12 feet (4m) is ideal and allows for the crane to work through the banister lifting things up and down! The cords are tied off with a length of nylon cord which is bound round and round — it looks much neater than knots.

I recommend that the whole crane is well varnished to give it adequate protection out of doors. A few touches of red paint on the cogs and jacks etc. add a finishing touch.

Quarry Crane Cutting List

Hopper Side Walls	2 off 209 × 121 × 9mm (8¼ × 4¾ × ⅜in) timber
Hopper End Walls	2 off 133 × 115 × 9mm (5¼ × 4½ × ⅜in) timber
Hopper Floor	1 off 133 × 127 × 9mm (5¼ × 5 × ⅜in) timber
Hopper Discharge Lever	1 off 175 × 50 × 20mm (7 × 2 × ¾in) timber
Lever Stops	2 off 25mm (1in) × 9mm (⅜in) diam dowel
Vertical Pulley Support	1 off 311 × 121 × 20mm (12¼ × 4¾ × ¾in) timber
Horizontal Pulley Support	1 off 342 × 95 × 20mm (13½ × 3¾ × ¾in) timber
Cab Sides	2 off 356 × 191 × 20mm (14 × 7½ × ¾in) timber
Cab Roof Panel	1 off 242 × 178 × 20mm (9½ × 7 × ¾in) timber
Upper Sloping Panel	1 off 178 × 121 × 20mm (7 × 4¾ × ¾in) timber
Lower Sloping Panel	1 off 178 × 38 × 20mm (7 × 1½ × ¾in) timber
Cab Front Panel	1 off 178 × 70 × 20mm (7 × 2¾ × ¾in) timber
Cab Floor Panel	1 off 356 × 178 × 20mm (14 × 7 × ¾in) timber
Cab Rear Panel	1 off 191 × 178 × 20mm (7½ × 7 × ¾in) timber
Winding Shafts	2 off 83mm (3¼in) × 16mm (⅝in) diam dowel
	2 off 242mm (9½in) × 16mm (⅝in) diam dowel
	1 off 95 × 95 × 20mm (3¾ × 3¾ × ¾in) timber
Jib Pivot Shaft	1 off 242mm (9½in) × 16mm (⅝in) diam dowel
	2 off 32 × 32 × 20mm (1¼ × 1¼ × ¾in) timber
Crane Base	2 off 851 × 89 × 20mm (33½ × 3½ × ¾in) timber
	2 off 273 × 89 × 20mm (10¾ × 3½ × ¾in) timber
	1 off 273 × 191 × 20mm (10¾ × 7½ × ¾in) timber
	2 off 273mm (10¾in) × 16mm (⅝in) diam dowel
Base Steady	4 off 286mm (11¼in) × 16mm (⅝in) diam dowel
	4 off 76 × 38 × 20mm (3 × 1½ × ¾in) timber
	4 off 38 × 38 × 20mm (1½ × 1½ × ¾in) timber
Jib Side Members	2 off 889 × 64 × 16mm (35 × 2½ × ⅝in) timber
Jib Stringers	16 off 95mm (3¾in) × 9mm (⅜in) diam dowel
Ratchet Wheel	2 off 51 × 51 × 20mm (2 × 2 × ¾in) timber
Ratchet	2 off 57 × 20 × 20mm (2¼ × ¾ × ¾in) timber
Lifting Block	1 off 83 × 83 × 20mm (3¼ × 3¼ × ¾in) timber
Jib Cross Member	1 off 95 × 44 × 20mm (3¾ × 1¾ × ¾in) timber
Ancillaries	4 off 89mm (3½in) diam pulleys
	1 off 102mm (4in) × 6mm (¼in) diam steel spindle
	2 off 108mm (4¼in) × 6mm (¼in) diam steel spindle
	6 off 6mm (¼in) spring dome caps
	2 off 9mm (⅜in) ^{o}/diam × 6mm (¼in) ^{i}/diam plastic spacers
	4 off 20mm (¾in) diam screwed eyes
	1 off 20mm (¾in) diam screwed hook
	1 off 2 metre (78in) strong red nylon cord
	1 off 2 metre (78in) strong green nylon cord
	1 off 64mm (2½in) × 9mm (⅜in) ^{o}/diam × 6mm (¼in) ^{i}/diam plastic spacer

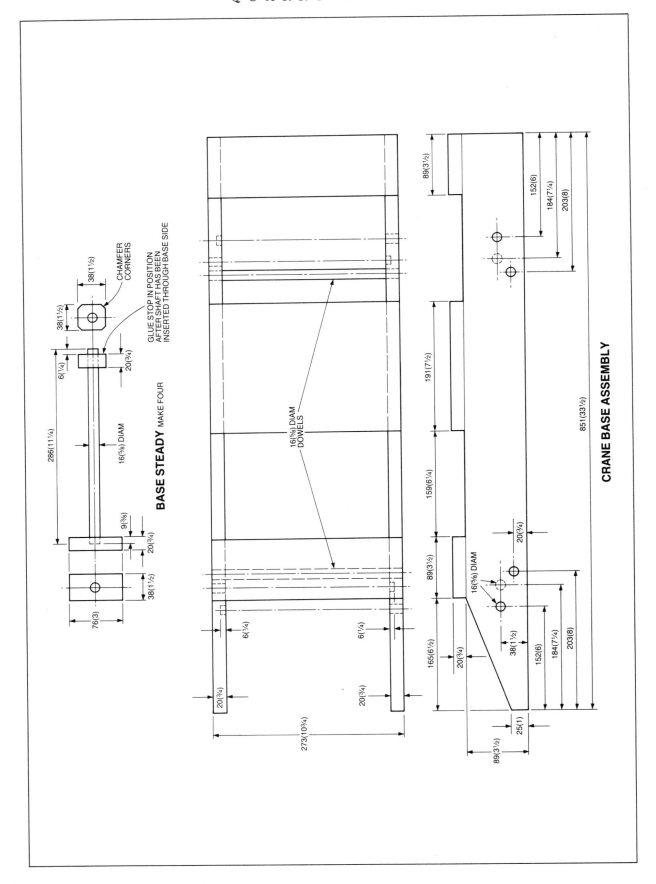

BASE STEADY MAKE FOUR

CHAMFER CORNERS

GLUE STOP IN POSITION AFTER SHAFT HAS BEEN INSERTED THROUGH BASE SIDE

38(1½)

38(1½)

6(¼)

20(¾)

286(11¼)

16(⅝) DIAM

9(⅜)

20(¾)

38(1½)

76(3)

CRANE BASE ASSEMBLY

16(⅝) DIAM DOWELS

89(3½)

152(6)

184(7¼)

203(8)

191(7½)

159(6¼)

89(3½)

851(33½)

165(6½)

20(¾)

16(⅝) DIAM

38(1½)

152(6)

184(7¼)

203(8)

20(¾)

25(1)

89(3½)

273(10¾)

6(¼)

6(¼)

20(¾)

20(¾)

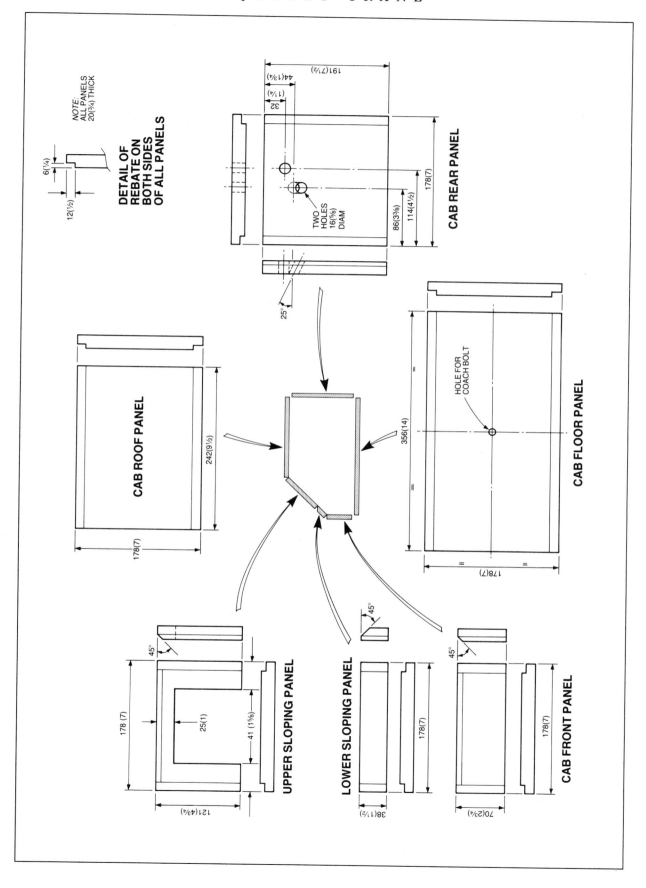

NOTE:
ALL PANELS
20(3/4) THICK

6(1/4)

12(1/2)

DETAIL OF
REBATE ON
BOTH SIDES
OF ALL PANELS

CAB REAR PANEL

191(7½)
44(1¾)
32(1¼)
178(7)
86(3⅜)
114(4½)
TWO HOLES 16(⅝) DIAM
25°

CAB ROOF PANEL
242(9½)
178(7)

CAB FLOOR PANEL
356(14)
178(7)
HOLE FOR COACH BOLT

UPPER SLOPING PANEL
45°
178(7)
25(1)
41(1⅝)
121(4¾)

LOWER SLOPING PANEL
45°
178(7)
38(1½)

CAB FRONT PANEL
45°
178(7)
70(2¾)

VERTICAL PULLEY SUPPORT ASSEMBLY

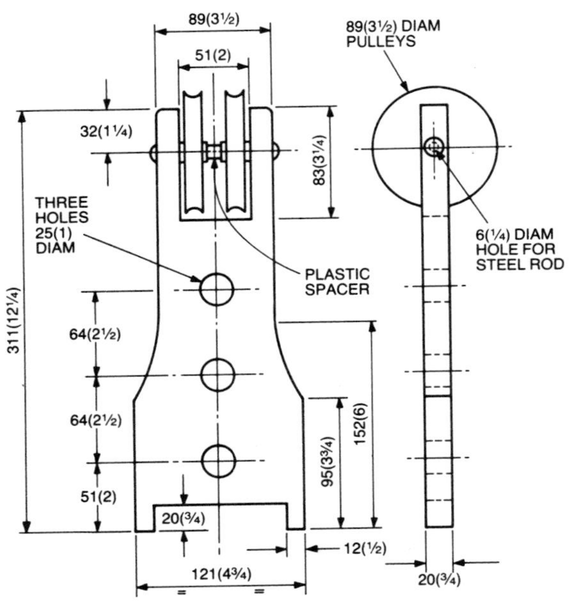
89(3½)
51(2)
89(3½) DIAM PULLEYS
32(1¼)
83(3¼)
THREE HOLES 25(1) DIAM
6(¼) DIAM HOLE FOR STEEL ROD
PLASTIC SPACER
311(12¼)
64(2½)
64(2½)
152(6)
95(3¾)
51(2)
20(¾)
12(½)
121(4¾)
20(¾)

HORIZONTAL PULLEY SUPPORT ASSEMBLY

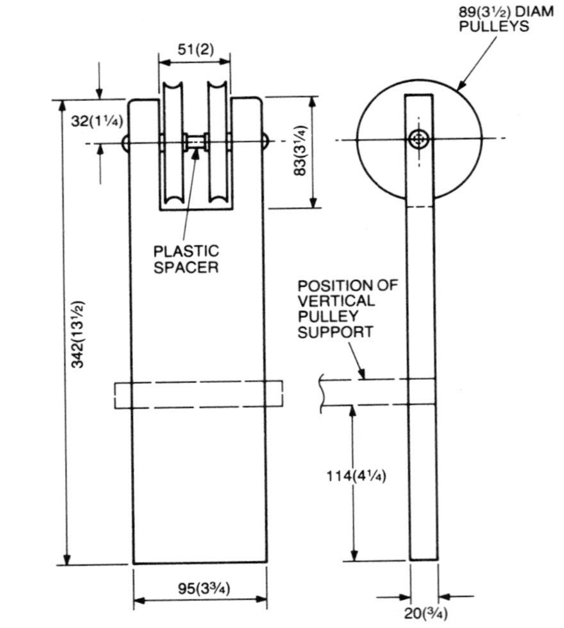
89(3½) DIAM PULLEYS
51(2)
32(1¼)
83(3¼)
PLASTIC SPACER
POSITION OF VERTICAL PULLEY SUPPORT
342(13½)
114(4¼)
95(3¾)
20(¾)

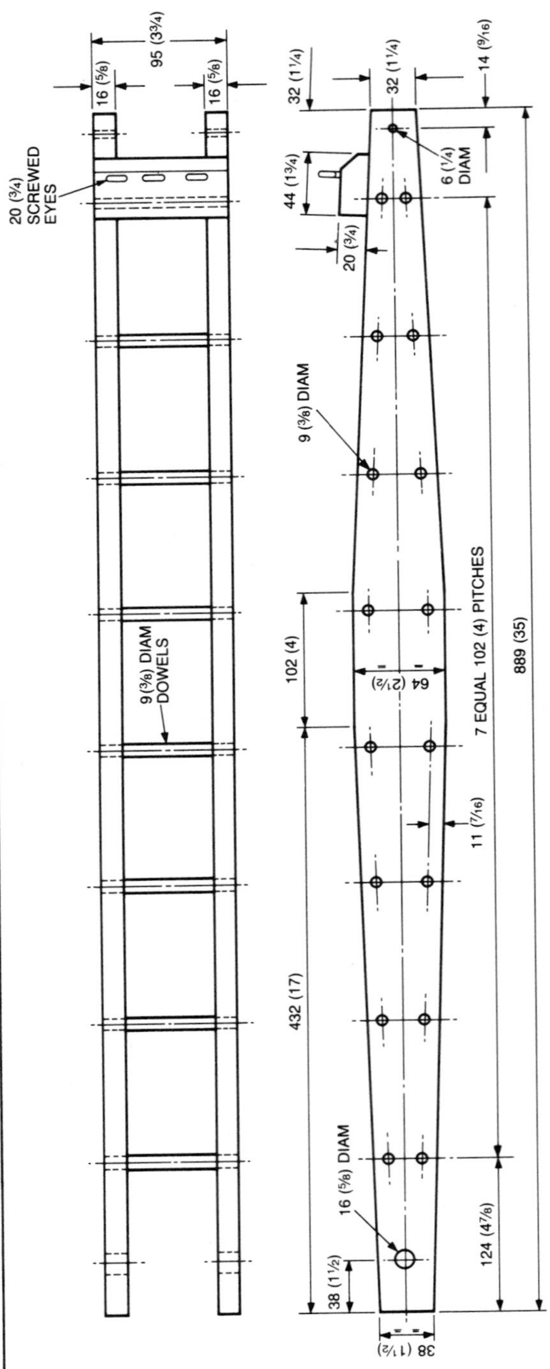
95 (3¾)
16 (⅝)
16 (⅝)
20 (¾) SCREWED EYES
9 (⅜) DIAM DOWELS
32 (1¼)
32 (1¼)
14 (9/16)
6 (¼) DIAM
44 (1¾)
20 (¾)
9 (⅜) DIAM
102 (4)
64 (2½)
7 EQUAL 102 (4) PITCHES
889 (35)
11 (7/16)
432 (17)
16 (⅝) DIAM
124 (4⅞)
38 (1½)
38 (1½)

JIB ASSEMBLY

1. TEDDY BEAR'S BUGGY – a versatile and robust 4-wheel push cart which is relatively easy to make and will provide hours of fun and games.

2. SCOOTA TRIKE – an excellent toy for a toddler. The trailer is useful for carrying teddy or the building bricks.

3. BUNK BEDS FOR TEDS – a simple project which enables teddy to be put through the punishment of going to bed – just like you!

4. WILF – a thoroughly articulated caterpillar with segments that move on two planes.

5. BLITZEN BENZ (1909) – a challenging project using those marvellous dark hardwoods. The smooth curves of the bonnet take a lot of finishing but, as you can see, it really is worth the effort.

6. GERMAN FOKKER TRIPLANE – a fabulous and challenging project to put you right up there with Red Baron.

7. COACHING IN STYLE – a Volvo luxury coach with mahogany trimmings and windscreen wipers made of wire and plastic tube painted black.

8. BARREL ORGAN – a fun project which makes a most attractive jewellery box at the same time.

9. MAN F90 LORRY – this impressive articulated vehicle won the European 'Truck of the Year Award' in 1987. The model is made from Brazilian mahogany and pine.

10. QUARRY CRANE – an exciting project involving a bucket, winch and stabilisers. Ideal for play in the garden or sandpit.

11. HORSE-DRAWN POST OFFICE VAN – a reminder of the days when parcel delivery was a more leisurely affair. The china horse determined the scale of the van.

12. MERCEDES BENZ 4-WHEEL DRIVE TRACTOR – this superb tractor is an excellent toy for use in small areas, perhaps even at play schools. It is sturdy and the additional trailer can be loaded with all kinds of trimming and debris.

13. TANK ENGINE AND COACHES – this striking and sturdy train is surprisingly straightforward to make. Any number of carriages can be added and there is plenty of scope for decorative paint-work.

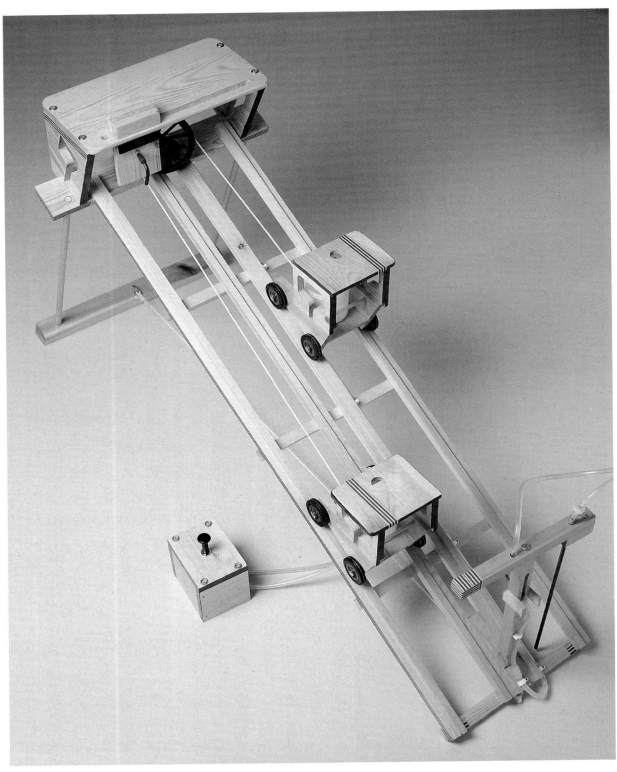

14. WATER-POWERED MOUNTAIN HOIST – this ingenious form of passenger transport is inspired by the Linton and Lynmouth Cliff Railway.

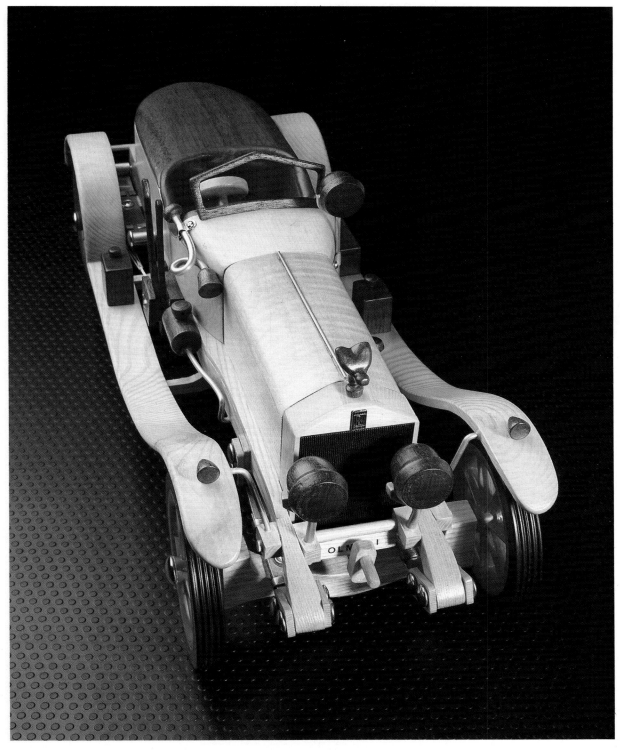

15. BOAT-TAILED SPORTING SILVER GHOST – this classic Rolls Royce is a more complex but thoroughly rewarding project. It is well worth paying close attention to the details such as the 'spirit of ecstasy' emblem which distinguishes the famous make.

16. WARD-LA-FRANCE RESCUE TRUCK – the official name for this massive American fire engine. This fabulous working model has an eight foot extending ladder and working water pumps.

17. MAN 6-WHEEL TIPPER TRUCK – a solid and finely built toy which will stand up to heavy loads and outdoor use. It is made from Nordic redwood with Brazilian mahogany finishes.

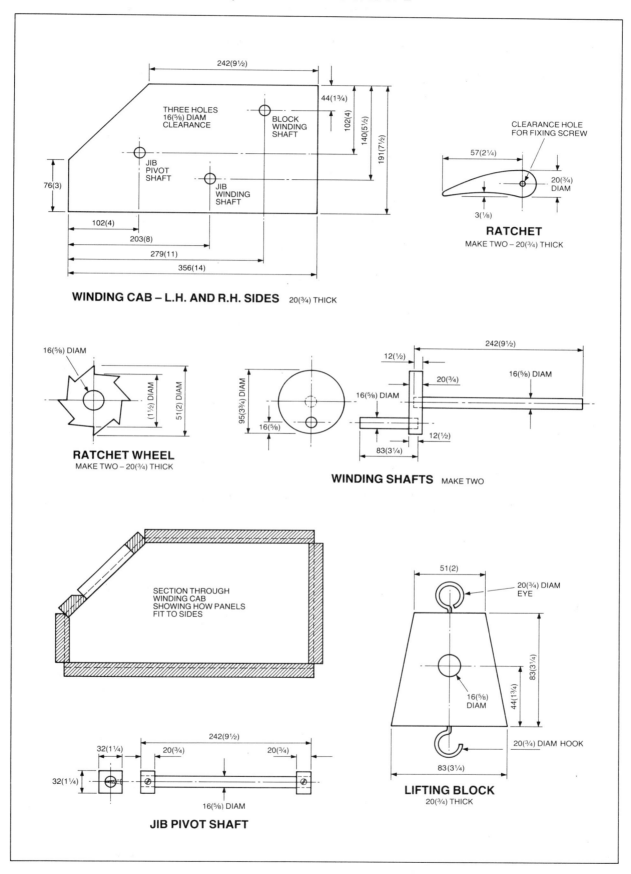

242(9½)

44(1¾)

102(4)

140(5½)

191(7½)

THREE HOLES
16(⅝) DIAM
CLEARANCE

BLOCK
WINDING
SHAFT

JIB
PIVOT
SHAFT

JIB
WINDING
SHAFT

76(3)

102(4)

203(8)

279(11)

356(14)

WINDING CAB – L.H. AND R.H. SIDES 20(¾) THICK

CLEARANCE HOLE
FOR FIXING SCREW

57(2¼)

20(¾)
DIAM

3(⅛)

RATCHET
MAKE TWO – 20(¾) THICK

16(⅝) DIAM

(1½) DIAM

51(2) DIAM

RATCHET WHEEL
MAKE TWO – 20(¾) THICK

12(½)

20(¾)

242(9½)

16(⅝) DIAM

95(3¾) DIAM

16(⅝) DIAM

16(⅝)

83(3¼)

12(½)

WINDING SHAFTS MAKE TWO

SECTION THROUGH
WINDING CAB
SHOWING HOW PANELS
FIT TO SIDES

51(2)

20(¾) DIAM
EYE

83(3¼)

44(1¾)

16(⅝)
DIAM

20(¾) DIAM HOOK

83(3¼)

LIFTING BLOCK
20(¾) THICK

32(1¼)

20(¾)

242(9½)

20(¾)

32(1¼)

16(⅝) DIAM

JIB PIVOT SHAFT

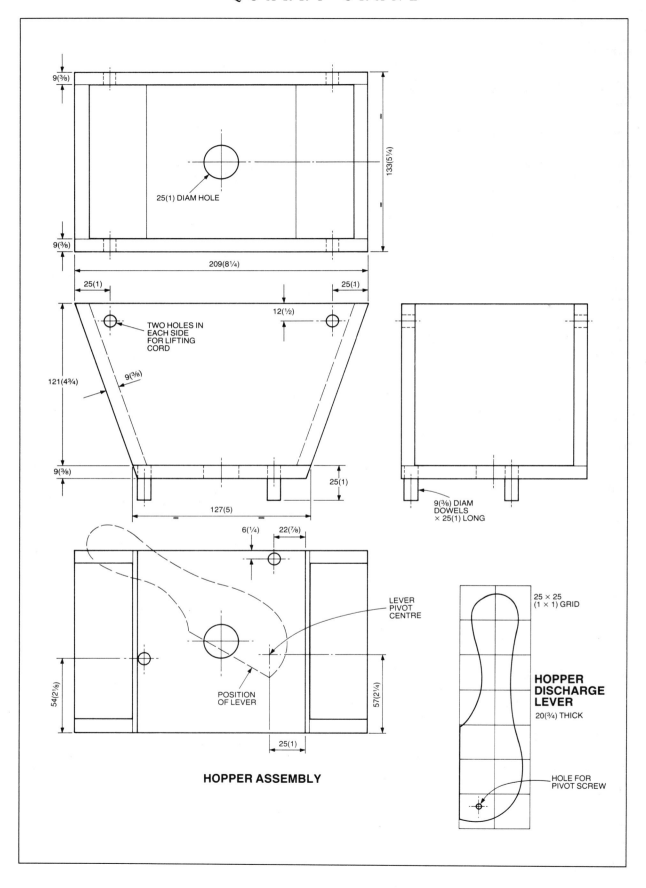

HOPPER ASSEMBLY

HOPPER DISCHARGE LEVER

HORSE DRAWN POST OFFICE VAN

(See colour plate 11)

Over the past decade there has been a great interest in modelling all kinds of horse drawn vehicles. I have been absolutely thrilled to see some of the beautiful work that has gone into crafting some of these wagons and stage coaches. Some craftsmen not only achieve the difficult task of making replica wooden wheels, but make every detail of the model to scale.

This Post Office van is my first attempt and a good exercise as a starter. I have attempted to model a 1938 GPO London Parcel Van by McNamara. Due to the scarcity of petrol during the Second World War these horse drawn vehicles were in great demand and could still be seen working as late as 1949. This van was fitted with pneumatic tyres, drum brakes and electric side lights.

TIMBER
The timber used is Nordic Redwood.

TO MAKE
1.   Start by making the front and rear axle assemblies. The marking out for the axle hole has to be done carefully from both ends. It is essential to keep both pieces of wood at 90 degrees in both planes when drilling the axle holes. The semicircular section on front and rear axles is removed after drilling the holes. You will find that a small coping saw will do this job well.

2.   The front and rear axle blocks are held on to the underside of the van by two different methods:

* The rear axle has two small pieces of wood glued on to the top edge in the 'cut outs' provided. This unit is then glued on to the underside of the van.

* The front axle needs to pivot. Drill a hole right through the centre of the axle to take a screw. At the top of the axle 'cut outs' are provided to take two lengths of wood that in turn provide the fixing place for the shafts. Glue these two lengths in place. In order to secure them firmly to the axle assembly, a further strip of wood is glued behind and beneath them.

3.   The shafts are not as difficult as they look, but it is best to buy a horse first before you do any cutting. I made paper templates of the shafts until I arrived at what seemed a good fit for my horse. However, do drill the hole at the back of the shaft before starting to cut out the curved section.

Then whittle away all the square edges [I used a chisel and Stanley knife] and finally finish off with glasspaper.

The front and rear axles are now complete and these are best put to one side before work starts on the van body.

4.   The floor of the van is simply a length of wood on to which the sides are glued. However, to make the joint stronger between the floor and the side, a rebate (L-shaped slot) is cut on the bottom edge of both sides. It is also a good idea to cut a rebate at the front edge. This rebate takes the front section which is glued into it. You can if you wish omit the rebates, but it won't be quite as strong.

5.   To allow the driver access, the sides have to be cut away. Cutting the curved opening at the front is done with a coping saw and afterwards the saw cuts removed with glasspaper.

6.   Cut the roof to shape and either use a Surform wood rasp or traditional plane to chamfer off the roof section at the front. All the edges must be carefully chamfered.

7.   The front bulkhead is shaped and the driver's seat glued into place. There are no 'joints' as such on this piece and on assembly the sides, top and bottom are simply glued into place.

8.   The door at the back is hinged; if you don't feel confident to fit small brass hinges then there is the quick and simple alternative of a pair of magnetic catches. These catches are readily available at DIY shops and work extremely well. They also have the advantage of being more robust than small hinges and are preferable if the toy is intended as a present. Final fitting of the door is left to last. The door handle is oversize and designed for little fingers to get a good grip.

9.   Once all the parts have been made, assemble it 'dry' (without glue) and see if all the pieces fit before going further. Glue the sides on to the base inserting the front bulkhead and the roof on to the sides. Now glue the section that acts as the driver's foot rest in place. Glue the various pieces of the front and rear axle together. Glue the rear axle into the base. Screw the front axle on to the base, leaving a very small amount of play for the axle to turn freely. Attach the shafts to the front axle either with a steel rod or dowel rod. Thread the axles through the holes and fit the rubber tyred wheels.

Horse Drawn Post Office Van Cutting List

Floor Assembly	1 off 304 × 165 × 20mm (12 × 6½ × ¾in) timber
	1 off 165 × 44 × 20mm (6½ × 1¾ × ¾in) timber
Front Axle Assembly	1 off 152 × 76 × 20mm (6 × 3 × ¾in) timber
	2 off 127 × 20 × 20mm (5 × ¾ × ¾in) timber
	1 off 152 × 20 × 20mm (6 × ¾ × ¾in) timber
Rear Axle Assembly	1 off 152 × 76 × 20mm (6 × 3 × ¾in) timber
	2 off 76 × 20 × 20mm (3 × ¾ × ¾in) timber
Shafts	1 off 250 × 150 × 20mm (10 × 6 × ¾in) timber
Sides	2 off 304 × 159 × 20mm (12 × 6¼ × ¾in) timber
Front Bulkhead	1 off 140 × 140 × 20mm (5½ × 5½ × ¾in) timber
	1 off 140 × 32 × 20mm (5½ × 1¼ × ¾in) timber
Roof	1 off 330 × 191 × 20mm (13 × 7½ × ¾in) timber
Rear Door	1 off 137 × 137 × 20mm (5⅜ × 5⅜ × ¾in) timber
	1 off 64 × 20 × 20mm (2½ × ¾ × ¾in) timber
Ancillaries	4 off 108mm (4½in) diam cart wheels
	2 off 197mm (7¾in) long × 6mm (¼in) diam steel axles
	1 off 164mm (6½in) long × 6mm (¼in) diam pivot pin
	6 off 6mm (¼in) spring dome caps

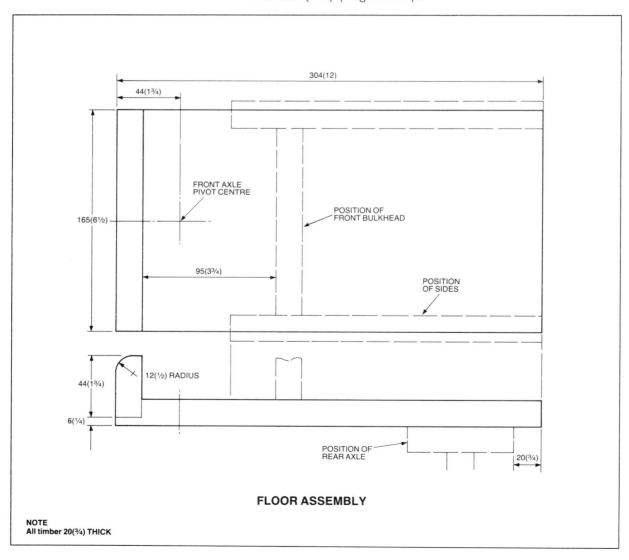

304(12)

44(1¾)

FRONT AXLE
PIVOT CENTRE

POSITION OF
FRONT BULKHEAD

165(6½)

95(3¾)

POSITION
OF SIDES

12(½) RADIUS

44(1¾)

6(¼)

POSITION OF
REAR AXLE

20(¾)

FLOOR ASSEMBLY

NOTE
All timber 20(¾) THICK

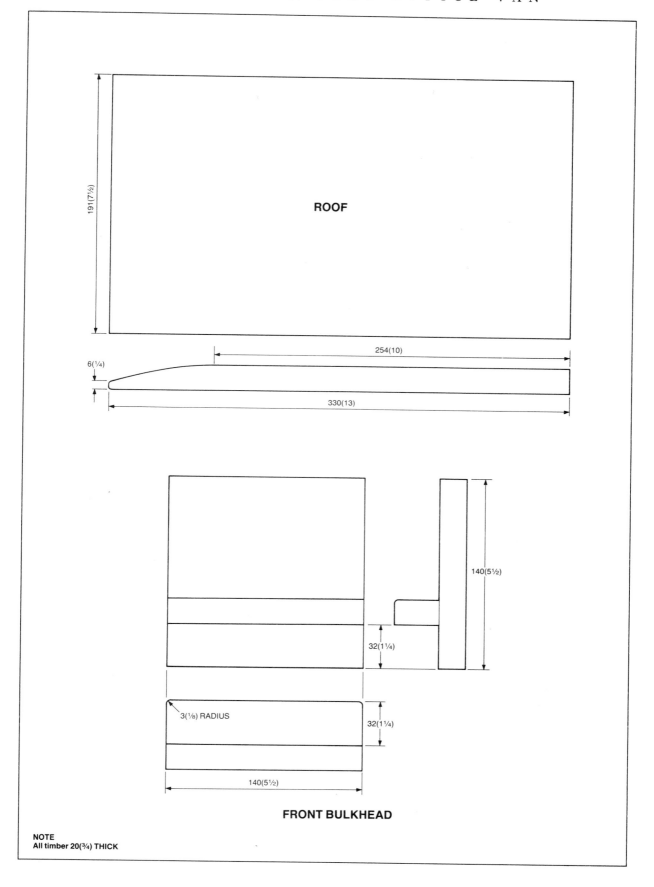

ROOF

191(7½)

254(10)

6(¼)

330(13)

140(5½)

32(1¼)

3(⅛) RADIUS

32(1¼)

140(5½)

FRONT BULKHEAD

NOTE
All timber 20(¾) THICK

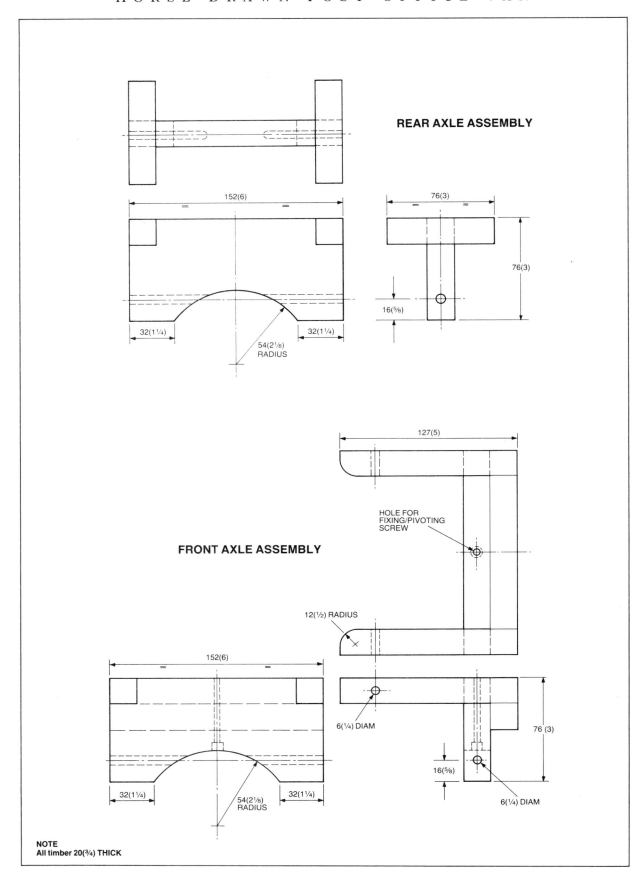

REAR AXLE ASSEMBLY

152(6)

76(3)

76(3)

16(⅝)

32(1¼)

32(1¼)

54(2⅛)
RADIUS

127(5)

HOLE FOR
FIXING/PIVOTING
SCREW

FRONT AXLE ASSEMBLY

12(½) RADIUS

152(6)

6(¼) DIAM

76 (3)

16(⅝)

32(1¼)

32(1¼)

54(2⅛)
RADIUS

6(¼) DIAM

NOTE
All timber 20(¾) THICK

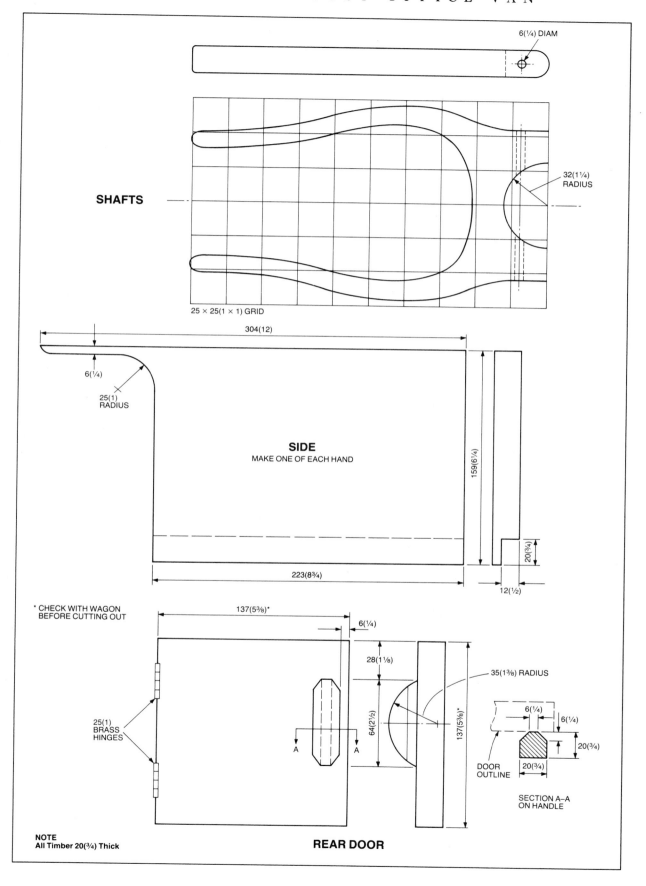

6(¼) DIAM

SHAFTS

32(1¼) RADIUS

25 × 25(1 × 1) GRID

304(12)

6(¼)

25(1) RADIUS

SIDE
MAKE ONE OF EACH HAND

159(6¼)

20(¾)

223(8¾)

12(½)

* CHECK WITH WAGON
BEFORE CUTTING OUT

137(5⅜)*

6(¼)

28(1⅛)

35(1⅜) RADIUS

25(1) BRASS HINGES

64(2½)

137(5⅜)*

6(¼)   6(¼)

20(¾)

A   A

DOOR OUTLINE

20(¾)

SECTION A–A
ON HANDLE

NOTE
All Timber 20(¾) Thick

REAR DOOR

61

MERCEDES BENZ 4-WHEEL DRIVE TRACTOR

(See colour plate 12)

With the harvest safely in, the farmer starts the Autumn ploughing. I find it an impressive sight to watch a 4-wheel drive tractor pulling a 6-furrow plough being followed by a host of gulls.

These 4-wheel drive Mercedes Benz tractors are superb machines and having all four wheels the same size is an added advantage when working on slippery field banks.

This is not a difficult model to build and is a convenient size for most bedrooms or playrooms.

TIMBER
The model is built from Nordic Redwood with the addition of a few pieces of Brazilian Mahogany to add a dash of colour.

TO MAKE
1. Work begins by marking and cutting out the tractor chassis. Shaping is done by cutting away pieces of wood from a standard stock size piece of soft wood. On the underside, recesses are cut to take front and back axles. The front axle recess has to be cut away at either side to allow room for the axle to pivot from the centre.

2. Front and rear axles are now made. It is important to drill the axle hole vertically at 90 degrees in both planes. To prevent a great deal of frustration it's a good idea to invest in a vertical drill stand. If you don't have a drill stand then be sure to mark out the chassis on both sides. Now drill the axle holes working from both sides of the chassis. Both front and back axles are chamfered off on their edges. The back axle is now glued into the chassis. The front axle is held to the chassis by a large screw that passes through the engine compartment. Don't forget to countersink the screw head.

3. The tow hitch is made and to give it strength both glued and screwed onto the underside of the chassis, butting up against the back axle.

4. The engine itself is represented by a block of shaped wood. This gives the keen modeller great scope for more details. In the top of the engine a hole is drilled to accommodate the exhaust stack which fits into this hole when the bonnet is fitted.

5. The front 'bumper' is now fitted. I have not attempted to detail the complicated linkage that is found in the real machine. Making the 'bumper'

from a contrasting piece of wood makes it look more sturdy. Before gluing the bumper in place, drill and fit the small dowel rod that acts as the location peg for the bottom of the radiator. The front headlights are made with a plug cutter.

6. Now mark out the cab sides and rear panel. The cab windows can be cut out by drilling a hole in the waste section, threading the coping saw blade through the hole (re-connecting the blade in the frame) and cutting around the window. Do keep the work low in the vice as this will help to reduce the vibration while sawing.

Use glasspaper to remove the saw cuts on the window frames. The back window of the cab is simply cut out with the coping saw and the cab roof functions as the top bar of the window.

7. The floor and front bulkhead of the cab are now made and the roof cut to shape. Drill a hole in the front bulkhead to take the steering wheel. Cut and fit both seat and steering wheel. Now glue the cab together. You will find that light cramps are ideal but the use of masking tape is a good substitute for holding things together while the glue dries. Glue the cab onto the chassis.

8. Now cut and fit the rear platform, gluing the top pieces of the mudguard assembly on. Screw heads always look ugly so counterbore the hole which will allow the screw head to go below the surface. Cut 2 wood plugs and glue over the tops of the screws. Trim off the plug when the glue is dry.

9. Shape the two front mudguards. This is a painstaking job as it is necessary to cut 60 degree mitres on the bottoms and tops of each. Once shaping is complete, glue the mudguards in place. The front mudguards are now completed by gluing small blocks on to the top edge. 2 small pieces of contrasting timber are now glued on to these to represent side lights.

10. To allow the driver ease of access to the cab, steps are fitted. The steps are glued to one side to the front mudguard and at the back to a supporting piece of timber that is glued on to the chassis and the underside of the cab. Angles have to be planed to get the steps to fit. This is the most difficult part of the job and you will need to give yourself a little time to get it right.

11. Now the back mudguards are fitted to the underside of the rear platform.

12. Now shape up the radiator and bonnet. This should be done with great care as it is this single feature that gives the true character to your toy. The radiator is glued on to the bonnet and side panels (contrasting wood) are then glued in place. Now work can begin on the grille. First cut and plane some very thin strips of wood. Following the drawing cut to size and glue on to the radiator. Now cut some aluminium mesh (used for car repair of rusty wings) and fit onto the radiator front. Now fit three small 'bars' of wood across the front to form the complete grille. These three bars hold the mesh in place.

The world famous Mercedes Badge was obtained from a key fob, which was then glued onto the three bars (epoxy resin glue). A piece of plastic tube (high tension ignition spark lead) is then fitted which lines up and goes right through the bonnet into the hole in the engine block below (a bit of very careful drilling needed at this stage).

A small hole is now drilled on the underside of the radiator which locates with the peg on the front bumper.

13. Contrasting pieces of wood are used for headlights, rear lights and door handles.

TRAILER

1. No tractor is complete without a trailer. Cut out the main chassis member and prepare the centre body supports and the back support that runs full width.

2. Cut and shape the front, back and back axles. The front axle swivels. Now to avoid unsightly screws projecting into the base of the trailer a counterbored hole is made in the front of the chassis. The screw is then inserted and goes straight into the front axle and hitch. It's worth doing the screw up fairly tightly as when the trailer body is fitted this screw is not accessible. Drill holes to take the steel rods and then fit the axle blocks to the main chassis.

3. The trailer base is now glued on to the chassis, and the centre body supports glued either side of the main chassis.

4. The trailer sides are fitted together with rebates. Now it's not essential to cut rebates, but it is definitely a far stronger joint than just 'butting' edges together with glue. A rebate plane or router are necessary to cut the 'L' shaped rebates.

Once the joints are cut the body sides are glued around the base. This job may take a bit of patient trimming with a plane to get the sides to fit neatly around the base.

5. Chamfer off the top of the trailer and all the corners. It's always easier to varnish or paint the toy before the wheels are fitted. However, remember to chamfer off the ends of the steel axle rods before fitting the wheels and pressing the spring caps on to the ends of the axles.

Mercedes Benz 4-Wheel Drive Tractor Cutting List

Chassis	1 off 336 × 83 × 44mm (13¼ × 3¼ × 1¾in) timber
Towing Hitch	1 off 76 × 44 × 16mm (3 × 1¾ × ⅝in) timber
	1 off 64mm (2½in) × 12mm (½in) diam dowel
Front and Rear Axles	2 off 117 × 44 × 44mm (4⅝ × 1¾ × 1¾in) timber
Steps	2 off 64 × 44 × 12mm (2½ × 1¾ × ½in) timber
	Make from 162 × 44 × 12mm (6⅜ × 1¾ × ½in) timber
Roof	1 off 140 × 105 × 12mm (5½ × 4⅛ × ½in) timber
	1 off 60 × 60 × 3mm (2⅜ × 2⅜ × ⅛in) timber
	2 off 12 × 12 × 6mm (½ × ½ × ¼in) timber
	2 off 25 × 5 × 3mm (1 × 3⁄16 ⅛in) timber
Front Mudguard	2 off 108 × 67 × 12mm (4¼ × 2⅝ × ½in) timber
	2 off 57 × 32 × 12mm (2¼ × 1¼ × ½in) timber
	2 off 25 × 9 × 3mm (1 × ⅜ × ⅛in) timber
Cab Side	2 off 108 × 94 × 12mm (4¼ × 3¹¹⁄16 × ½in) timber
Rear Panel	1 off 105 × 96 × 12mm (4⅛ × 3¾ × ½in) timber
Floor	1 off 105 × 79 × 12mm (4⅛ × 3⅛ × ½in) timber
Front Bulkhead	1 off 105 × 44 × 12mm (4⅛ × 1¾ × ½in) timber
Steering Wheel	1 off 6mm (¼in) × 25mm (1in) diam dowel
	1 off 38mm (1½in) × 5mm (3⁄16in) diam dowel
Seat	1 off 64 × 44 × 38mm (2½ × 1¾ × 1½in) timber
Door Handle	2 off 20 × 5 × 3mm (¾ × 3⁄16 × ⅛in) timber

Mercedes Benz 4-Wheel Drive Tractor Cutting List *continued*

Engine Bonnet	1 off 121 × 67 × 16mm (4¾ × 2⅝ × ⅝in) timber
	1 off 92 × 70 × 56mm (3⅝ × 2¾ × 2³⁄₁₆in) timber
Radiator	1 off 72 × 70 × 16mm (2¹³⁄₁₆ × 2¾ × ⅝in) timber
Air Intake	1 off 6mm (¼in) × 12mm (½in) diam dowel
Radiator Grille	Make from 241 × 5 × 5mm (9½ × ³⁄₁₆ × ³⁄₁₆in) timber
Radiator Badge	1 off 5mm (³⁄₁₆in) × 32mm (1¼in) diam
Front Bumper	1 off 95 × 32 × 16mm (3¾ × 1¼ × ⅝in) timber
	2 off 6mm (¼in) × 12mm (½in) diam dowel
	1 off 12mm (½in) × 6mm (¼in) diam dowel
Engine	1 off 44 × 38 × 38mm (1¾ × 1½ × 1½in) timber
Rear Platform	1 off 159 × 130 × 12mm (6¼ × 5⅛ × ½in) timber
	2 off 130 × 32 × 12mm (5⅛ × 1¼ × ½in) timber
	4 off 57 × 38 × 12mm (2¼ × 1½ × ½in) timber
	2 off 32 × 9 × 3mm (1¼ × ⅜ × ⅛in) timber
Ancillaries	8 off 102mm (4in) diam road wheels
	2 off 240mm (9½in) × 6mm (¼in) diam steel axles
	4 off 6mm (¼in) spring dome caps
	1 off 64mm (2½in) × 64mm (2½in) expanded steel mesh
	1 off 102mm (4in) × 6mm (¼in) diam rubber

Tractor Trailer Cutting List

Base	1 off 336 × 159 × 16mm (13¼ × 6¼ × ⅝in) timber
Side Panels	2 off 368 × 95 × 16mm (14½ × 3¾ × ⅝in) timber
Front and Rear Panels	2 off 178 × 95 × 16mm (7 × 3¾ × ⅝in) timber
Main Chassis	1 off 314 × 44 × 44mm (12⅜ × 1¾ × 1¾in) timber
Rear Body Support	1 off 191 × 32 × 16mm (7½ × 1¼ × ⅝in) timber
Centre Body Support	4 off 73 × 32 × 16mm (2⅞ × 1¼ × ⅝in) timber
Rear Axle	1 off 140 × 44 × 44mm (5½ × 1¾ × 1¾in) timber
Front Axle and Hitch	1 off 140 × 44 × 44mm (5½ × 1¾ × 1¾in) timber
	1 off 133 × 57 × 16mm (5¼ × 2¼ × ⅝in) timber
Ancillaries	4 off 102mm (4in) diam road wheels
	2 off 203mm (8in) × 6mm (¼in) diam steel axles
	4 off 6mm (¼in) spring dome caps

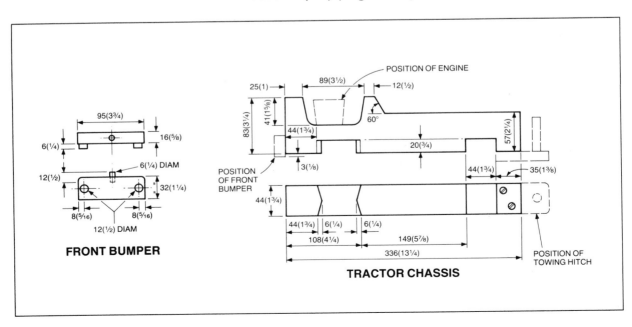

FRONT BUMPER

TRACTOR CHASSIS

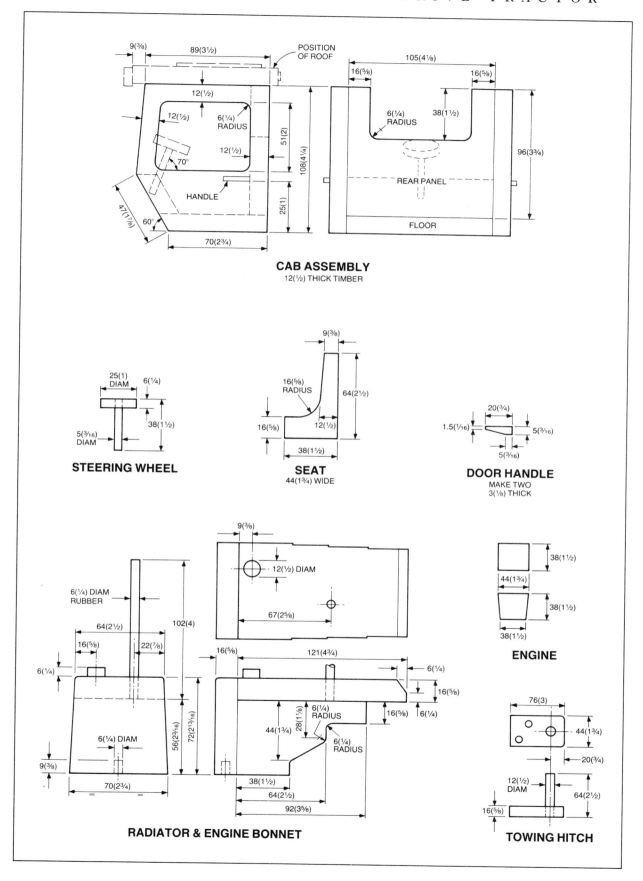

CAB ASSEMBLY
12(½) THICK TIMBER

STEERING WHEEL

SEAT
44(1¾) WIDE

DOOR HANDLE
MAKE TWO
3(⅛) THICK

ENGINE

RADIATOR & ENGINE BONNET

TOWING HITCH

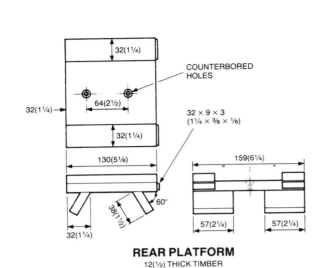

REAR PLATFORM
12(½) THICK TIMBER

ROOF

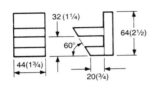

STEPS MAKE TWO
12(½) THICK TIMBER

SECTION A–A

RADIATOR BADGE
ACTUAL SIZE

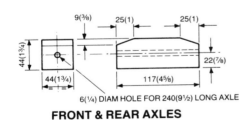

6(¼) DIAM HOLE FOR 240(9½) LONG AXLE

FRONT & REAR AXLES

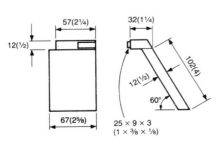

FRONT MUDGUARD
MAKE ONE OF EACH HAND

RADIATOR GRILLE
5(³⁄₁₆) THICK

THREE STRIPS
3(⅛) WIDE

EXPANDED
MESH

TRAILER

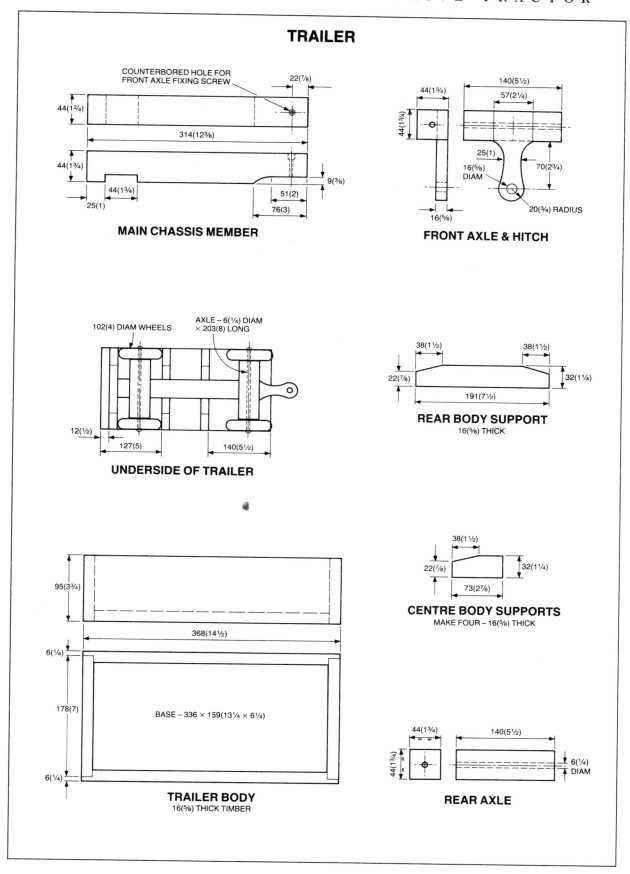

MAIN CHASSIS MEMBER

FRONT AXLE & HITCH

UNDERSIDE OF TRAILER

REAR BODY SUPPORT
16(⅝) THICK

CENTRE BODY SUPPORTS
MAKE FOUR – 16(⅝) THICK

TRAILER BODY
16(⅝) THICK TIMBER

REAR AXLE

TANK ENGINE AND COACHES

(See colour plate 13)

This pocket-sized tank engine is an ideal 'first' to make for any youngster who you wish to 'play trains' with!

TIMBER
The wood used is Nordic Redwood and the timber used is stock size from most timber merchants.

TO MAKE
1. Make a start by shaping the body section of the tank engine. Using a tenon or hand saw make the vertical cut at the front of the cab and then turn the wood round in the vice to make the cut along what will be the top of the boiler. Make one more vertical cut at the front and then an angled cut to form the cowcatcher on the front. These saw cuts are pretty basic and should present no real problems.

2. Drill holes for the chimney, steam dome and, (changing the drill bit size) the holes for the wheels. Dowel rod is used for the chimney, but do chamfer the edges, it looks neater and removes sharp corners.

3. Cut out and shape up the side tanks and roof, these are then glued in place.

4. The hook at the back needs to have a really good length of threaded section otherwise it will just pull out and cause the driver great frustration. I discovered that the really strong hooks and eyes found in a good ironmongers are best.

THE COACHES
Any railway engine needs a good train of coaches. The method of construction is exactly the same for all three. You will find that its far easier to mark out three coaches on to one length of wood — do all the cutting and shaping in one operation and then cut off each carriage for the finishing operations.

1. The passenger accommodation radiused centres should be marked with a bradawl so that when it comes to the drilling stage it gives the drill bit a good start. Now using a flat bit, (in an electric drill) bore the holes out. It is of tremendous help to have a vertical drill stand to keep things at 90 degrees in both places while you drill. Drill all the axle holes.

2. Using a tenon saw cut vertically from the top downwards to the hole that forms the bottom of the passenger accommodation. Two vertical saw cuts are needed to remove the waste wood to form one passenger compartment. The same operation is repeated on all three carriages. Using a piece of glasspaper wrapped around a dowel rod remove all saw and drill marks from each compartment.

3. Separate the individual carriages and shape all the roof sections. Cut and shape the small running boards. Now glue roofs and running boards in place.

4. You will need to fit screw hooks and eyes alternately so that the train can be coupled up to the engine. Fit the wheels remembering that spring caps will only fit on the ends of steel axles if you have filed a chamfer on the end of each axle end.

5. The cream colour of the wood does need off-setting with a little red paint. To achieve this I painted the cowcatcher, chimney top and outside edges of the running boards. You can use red insulation tape if you prefer — its easier to use than paint. If paint is used, make sure it's non-toxic.

Tank Engine and Coaches Cutting List

Engine Body	1 off 241 × 92 × 44mm (9½ × 3⅝ × 1¾in) timber
Side Tanks	2 off 136 × 32 × 20mm (5⅜ × 1¼ × ¾in) timber
Cab Roof	1 off 92 × 86 × 20mm (3⅝ × 3⅜ × ¾in) timber
Funnel	1 off 57mm (2¼in) × 22mm (⅞in) diam dowel
Dome	1 off 38mm (1½in) × 16mm (⅝in) diam dowel
Ancillaries	6 off 51mm (2in) diam road wheels
	3 off 76mm (3in) long × 5mm (3/16in) diam steel axles
	6 off 5mm (3/16in) spring dome caps
	1 off 22mm (⅞in) diam screwed hook
Passenger Coach Body	1 off 254 × 92 × 44mm (10 × 3⅝ × 1¾in) timber
Running Boards	2 off 114 × 20 × 12mm (4½ × ¾ × ½in) timber
Roof	1 off 274 × 76 × 20mm (10¾ × 3 × ¾in) timber
Ancillaries	4 off 51mm (2in) diam road wheels
	2 off 76mm (3in) long × 5mm (3/16in) diam steel axles
	4 off 5mm (3/16in) spring dome caps
	1 off 22mm (⅞in) diam screwed hook
	1 off 22mm (⅞in) diam screwed eye

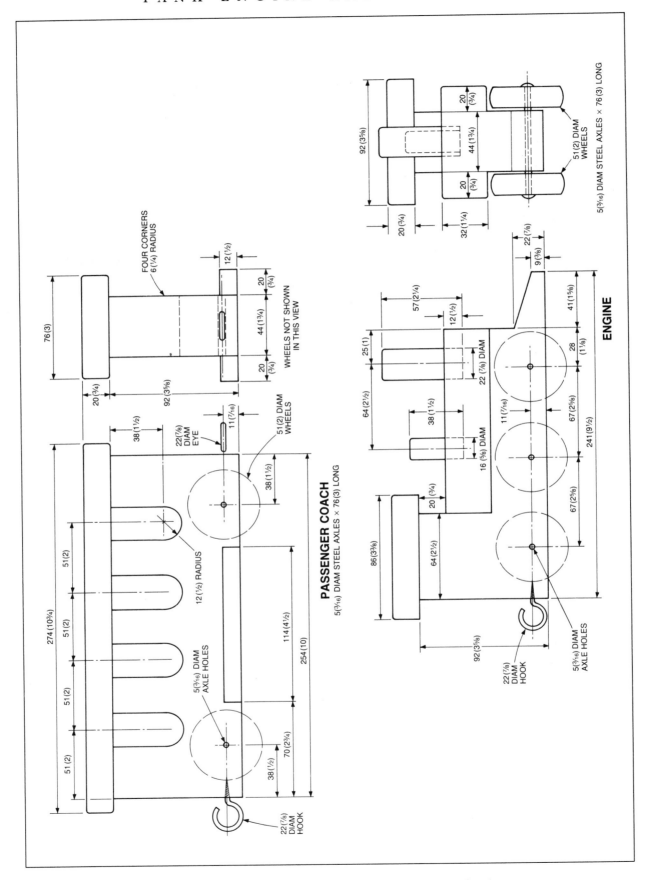

PASSENGER COACH
5(³/₁₆) DIAM STEEL AXLES × 76(3) LONG

ENGINE

WATER-POWERED MOUNTAIN RAILWAY

(See colour plate 14)

The inspiration to build this toy came from watching two small passenger carriages moving up and down the cliffs in the North Devon holiday town of Lynmouth.

The twin towns of Lynton and Lynmouth are linked by a cliff railway which uses water as its source of energy. At the top of the cliff railway, water is allowed to enter a huge tank on the bottom of the carriage. When the passengers are all in, a bell code system is used by the drivers and the driver at the bottom (Lynmouth) allows water to escape from his carriage. The carriage at the top is now heavier and the top carriage starts to move down the rails. The two carriages are connected by a steel hawser therefore as the top carriage moves down the one at the bottom moves up. There is an ingenious governor system to control the speed at which the carriages move. Not only is this water mountain railway worth a visit and a ride, but also one must salute the Victorian engineers who built it and those who maintain and operate it today.

This toy works on exactly the same principal, the only difference being that the water from the bottom carriage is re-cycled and pumped back to the top – well it does help to keep the house dry!

TIMBER
The timber used is Nordic Redwood.

TO MAKE
1. The inclined track consists of four strips of wood held together by four cross pieces that are screwed on to the track from the underside and at the top cabin, the trackway is secured to the floor with screws. The track itself has to be rebated (L-shaped groove on one side) on its two outer edges. The rebate has to be cut with a rebate plane or for those with an electric router the job is easily completed. However if you possess neither of these expensive tools then a visit to a hardware shop to buy some curtain track is the easiest way out. Plastic tracking can easily be fitted and the toy will work just as well. Using the cross pieces screw the tracking together.

2. In order to move the water from the bottom carriage into the top one, it is necessary to make a suction pipe assembly. The assembly fits between the two tracks and the top section swivels to allow the suction tube to go from one carriage to the other. The upright section of the assembly is glued in between the two tracks and blocks glued and fitted at either end. The cut out slot in the upright section allows the wheel axle ends to pass by without fouling the post. The metal tube must slide easily up and down in its retaining hole and is best made from copper or aluminium.

3. The cabin at the top is held in place by two dowel rods that connect to the track support below. The track support is tensioned by a length of nylon cord which is tied to the bottom of the inclined track. The tension in the cord keeps the whole structure taut. This method means that the track support and tracking can be folded away after play.

4. Cut out two cabin end walls. The doorways can be cut out with a coping saw. The roof has a slot to accommodate the water feed spout. Drill a hole at each end of the slot, slip the coping saw blade into the hole and with the roof held in the vice, saw from one hole along to the other. Repeat the operation for the other side.

With the waste wood removed from the slot, wrap a piece of glasspaper around an offcut of wood and paper the slot, removing all the saw cuts.

The cabin sides are now glued and screwed on to the track support at the top. The roof is screwed on to the sides. Use cup washers under the screw heads – they look so much better.

5. The water feed spout is now made from a piece of tubing – copper or aluminium is best for this. The wood slider holds the spout and is fitted into the roof slot before the side pieces are glued to the top. The two extra pieces glued to the slider at the top and one underneath the roof, prevent the slider from slipping out of the slot. The water feed spout and slot are essential as the carriage coming up the track is empty and therefore to fill the water container in it you must re-position the water supply to fill the empty carriage.

6. The large pulley wheel at the top is held in place with a long screw. It is essential to fit a spacer, (a piece of large diameter plastic tube) to line up the centre of the pulley wheel with the cord from the two carriages. Make sure that the wheel turns easily, it is vital that there is no friction otherwise it will not work.

7. Mark out the car body sides. Before shaping takes place, rebates are cut out on the inside edges. Cut out the windows at the sides. The car chassis is

now marked out. The sides are best cut out as pairs and the holes for the dowel rods and axle holes drilled while the chassis sides are together. The floor pieces are now made and glued on to the sides. Glue the dowel rods into place, using tape, strong elastic bands or light cramps to hold the pieces together while the glue cures (dries).

Fit the car body sides and the roof not forgetting to drill the hole in the roof to take the suction pump tube.

8. A small box is now made with one open side. The pump housing is a simple box that is glued together. In the top, drill a hole to take the pump body.

9. Before fitting tubes, wheels or any of the accessories varnish the complete toy. It's a good idea to apply three coats of varnish as this toy will get very wet. The carriages are lines with red paint. For the sides of the inclined track I used a decorative, self adhesive tape – it adds a touch of colour and is far easier than using paint.

FINAL ASSEMBLY
Fit the wheels on to both the carriages. Make sure that all wheels run freely (a squirt of WD40 will ensure this). Make certain that the pulley wheel at the top turns smoothly. Attach a length of nylon cord between the two cars and check that the cars run smoothly up and down each track way. Fit the two plastic water containers into the cars – retaining the plastic tops, but don't forget to bore holes in them.

Fit the leg stand and tie the nylon cord in place. A cup hook in the track support base makes it far easier to attach the nylon cord.

WATER PIPELINE
This is not as difficult as it looks. On to the top of the water suction pipe a non-return valve is fitted, (see *accessories* on page 00) the plastic tubing needs sufficient play for the pipe to be swivelled to the other track. From here the pipe is threaded through the swivel arm and into the upright arm. A piece of copper tube is used here to join the pipe together. The pipe now runs on the inside of the track. I found that the plastic clips used by electricians are ideal to hold the tubing in place. Take the nail from the clip and replace it with a chrome plated screw – it makes a very tidy method of fastening the tubing.

The tube now goes to the pump where it is fitted with another non-return valve. Another valve is fitted on the 'out going' side and the tube runs from here back up the cabin roof and then to the water feed spout. Fit another non return valve before attaching the tubing to the spout. The use of valves allows water in the system only to pass one way while it is being activated by the plunger in the pump body. By studying the illustrations you can see which way the valves have to be fitted. The system has initially to be primed (filled with water). If you have fitted one of the valves in the wrong direction it simply won't pump. The solution is to go back and check all the valves.

For wheels, axles, pumps and valves please see *Useful addresses* on page 00.

Water-Powered Mountain Railway Cutting List

Car Side	4 off 102 × 95 × 12mm (4 × 3¾ × ½in) timber
Car Roof	2 off 137 × 108 × 8mm (5⅜ × 4¼ × ⁵⁄₁₆in) timber
	2 off 97 × 20 × 8mm (3¾ × ¾ × ⁵⁄₁₆in) timber
Body	4 off 152 × 102 × 12mm (6 × 4 × ½in) timber
	6 off 108mm (4¼in) × 6mm (¼in) diam dowel
	2 off 95 × 83 × 12mm (3¾ × 3¼ × ½in) timber
Inclined Track Tie Bars	4 off 305 × 20 × 20mm (12 × ¾ × ¾in) timber
Track Rail	4 off 1168 × 25 × 20mm (46 × 1 × ¾in) timber
Header	1 off 457 × 67 × 20mm (18 × 2⅝ × ¾in) timber
Track Support	2 off 540mm (21¼in) × 12mm (½in) diam dowel
	1 off 457 × 64 × 41mm (18 × 2½ × 1⅝in) timber
Cabin End Wall	2 off 175 × 140 × 12mm (6⅞ × 5½ × ½in) timber
Cabin Roof	1 off 356 × 191 × 6mm (14 × 7½ × ¼in) timber
Water Feed Spout	1 off 137 × 83 × 11mm (5⅜ × 3¼ × ⁷⁄₁₆in) timber
	2 off 83 × 25 × 12mm (3¼ × 1 × ½in) timber
	1 off 83 × 20 × 9mm (3¼ × ¾ × ⅜in) timber
Pump House	1 off 127 × 89 × 12mm (5 × 3½ × ½in) timber
	2 off 95 × 89 × 12mm (3¾ × 3½ × ½in) timber
	1 off 103 × 95 × 12mm (4 × 3¾ × ½in) timber

Water-Powered Mountain Railway Cutting List *continued*

Suction Pipe Assembly
- 1 off 332 × 25 × 20mm (13⅛ × 1 × ¾in) timber
- 1 off 254 × 25 × 20mm (10 × 1 × ¾in) timber
- 1 off 57 × 25 × 20mm (2¼ × 1 × ¾in) timber
- 1 off 120 × 25 × 20mm (4¾ × 1 × ¾in) timber
- 2 off 44 × 20 × 9mm (1¾ × ¾ × ⅜in) timber

Ancillaries
- 8 off 51mm (2in) diam road wheels
- 4 off 143mm (5⅝in) × 6mm (¼in) diam steel axles
- 8 off 6mm (¼in) spring dome caps
- 1 off 127mm (5in) diam pulley wheel
- 1 off 3 metres (120in) strong nylon cord
- 1 off 25mm (1in) × 5mm (³⁄₁₆in) diam plastic spacer
- 1 off 25mm (1in) diam screwed hook
- 1 off Manual pump
- 1 off 2 metres (80in) plastic hose
- 4 off Non return valves
- 2 off 40mm (1⅝in) × 6mm (¼in) diam copper or
  aluminium tube
- 1 off 368mm (14½in) × 6mm (¼in) diam copper or
  aluminium tube
- 6 off Plastic hose clips
- 3 off Water tanks

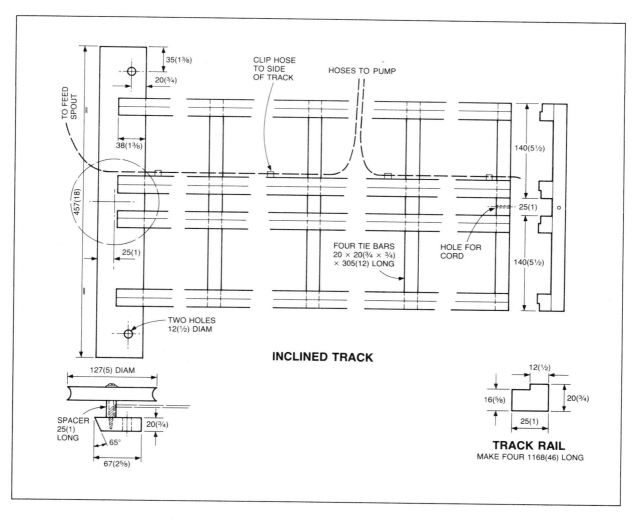

INCLINED TRACK

TRACK RAIL
MAKE FOUR 1168(46) LONG

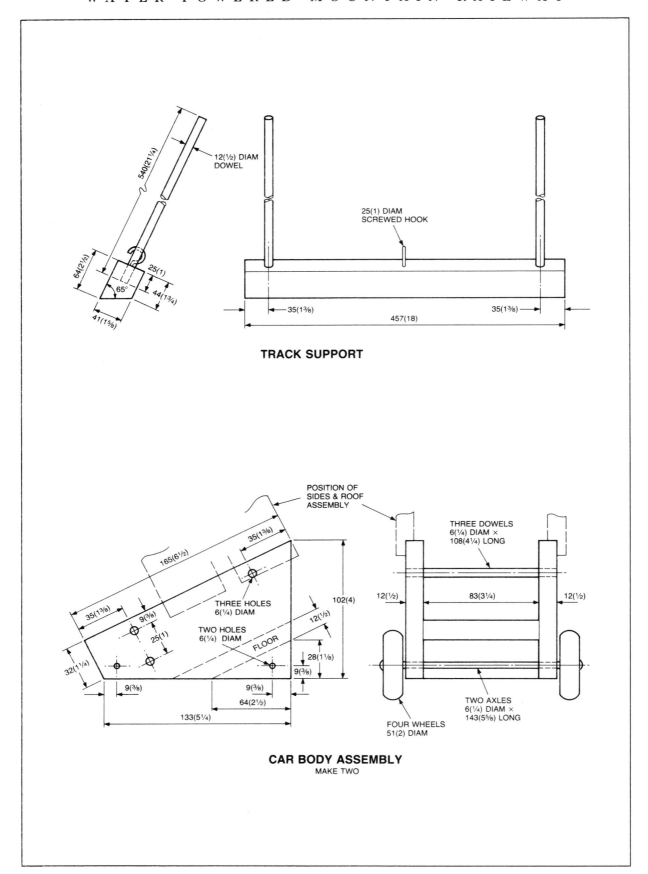

TRACK SUPPORT

CAR BODY ASSEMBLY
MAKE TWO

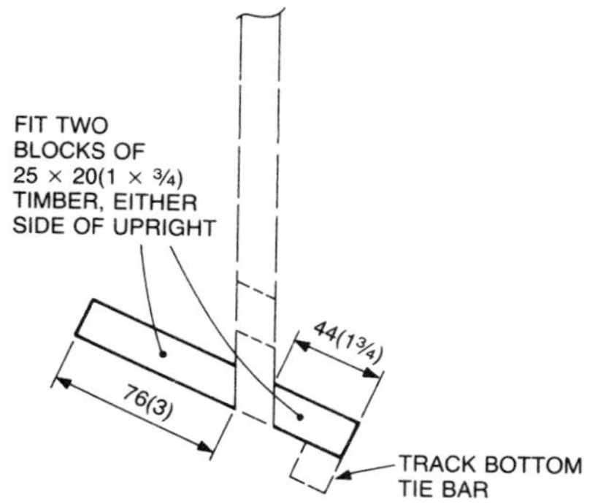
FIT TWO
BLOCKS OF
25 × 20(1 × ¾)
TIMBER, EITHER
SIDE OF UPRIGHT
44(1¾)
76(3)
TRACK BOTTOM
TIE BAR

MOUNTING DETAIL

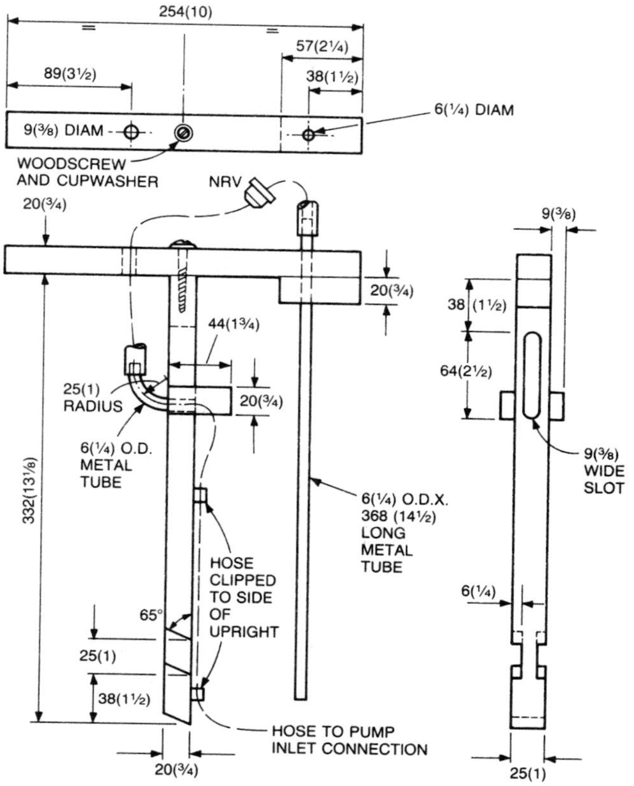
254(10)
57(2¼)
89(3½)
38(1½)
6(¼) DIAM
9(⅜) DIAM
WOODSCREW
AND CUPWASHER
NRV
20(¾)
9(⅜)
20(¾)
38 (1½)
44(1¾)
64(2½)
25(1)
RADIUS
20(¾)
6(¼) O.D.
METAL
TUBE
9(⅜)
WIDE
SLOT
332(13⅛)
6(¼) O.D.X.
368 (14½)
LONG
METAL
TUBE
HOSE
CLIPPED
TO SIDE
OF
UPRIGHT
6(¼)
65°
25(1)
38(1½)
HOSE TO PUMP
INLET CONNECTION
20(¾)
25(1)

SUCTION PIPE ASSEMBLY

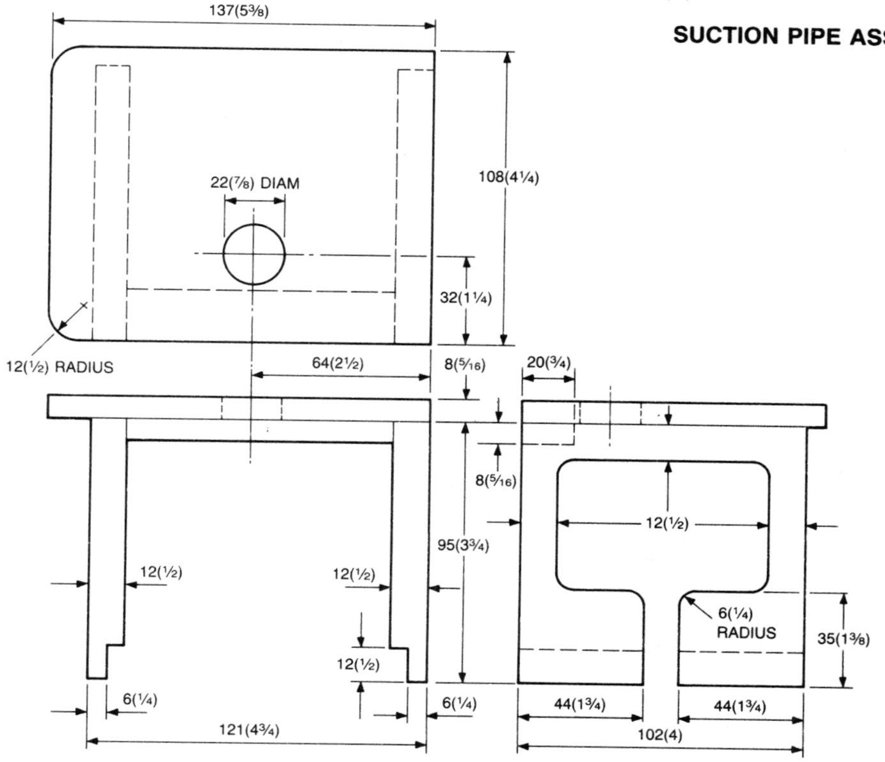
137(5⅜)
108(4¼)
22(⅞) DIAM
32(1¼)
12(½) RADIUS
64(2½)
8(5/16)
20(¾)
8(5/16)
12(½)
95(3¾)
12(½)
12(½)
6(¼)
RADIUS
35(1⅜)
12(½)
6(¼)
6(¼)
44(1¾)
44(1¾)
121(4¾)
102(4)

CAR SIDES AND ROOF ASSEMBLY

MAKE ONE OF EACH HAND

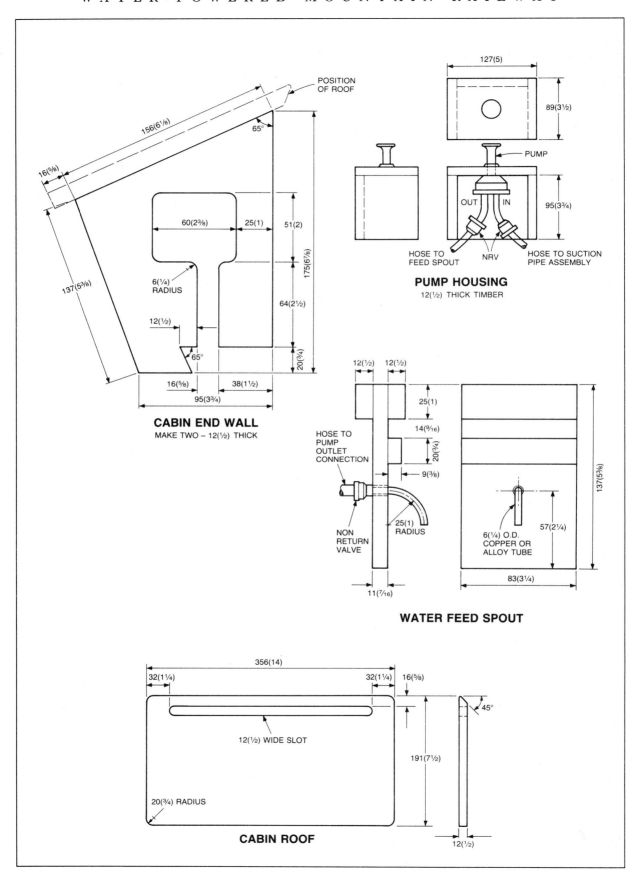

POSITION OF ROOF

156(6⅛)

65°

16(⅝)

137(5⅜)

60(2⅜)

25(1)

51(2)

175(6⅞)

6(¼) RADIUS

64(2½)

12(½)

65°

20(¾)

16(⅝)

38(1½)

95(3¾)

CABIN END WALL
MAKE TWO – 12(½) THICK

127(5)

89(3½)

PUMP

95(3¾)

OUT   IN

HOSE TO FEED SPOUT

NRV

HOSE TO SUCTION PIPE ASSEMBLY

PUMP HOUSING
12(½) THICK TIMBER

12(½)   12(½)

25(1)

14(9/16)

20(¾)

9(⅜)

HOSE TO PUMP OUTLET CONNECTION

25(1) RADIUS

NON RETURN VALVE

11(7/16)

137(5⅜)

6(¼) O.D. COPPER OR ALLOY TUBE

57(2¼)

83(3¼)

WATER FEED SPOUT

356(14)

32(1¼)

32(1¼)

16(⅝)

45°

12(½) WIDE SLOT

191(7½)

20(¾) RADIUS

12(½)

CABIN ROOF

BOAT-TAILED SPORTING SILVER GHOST

(See colour plate 15)

In my library I have a number of books that illustrate some of the world's most rare and beautiful cars. While looking through *Rolls Royce* by George Bishop published by Colour Library Books, I discovered a most beautiful 1912 Sporty 2-Seater Silver Ghost. Now sometimes I see machines that I feel instantly attracted to – this was one of those occasions and my reaction was, build it I must.

I contacted a number of Rolls Royce owners but I could not find where the car was or who owned it. So from the one picture in the book (page 18) I started work. If the owner of this magnificent machine ever reads this article I am sorry but without pictures I was unable to add accurate details for the driver's side of the car.

I should add that this is not a good first wookworking project and that in writing the instructions I have had to assume a fair amount of woodworking knowledge.

TIMBER

I used ash for the chassis, running boards, bonnet etc. The boat tail, fuel tank, dash board, headlamps and flying lady are all made from Brazilian mahogany. There are many other rare and beautiful timbers to choose from but these are two of my favourites.

TO MAKE

1. The chassis side members are the first job to tackle. The chassis on these models curved in at the engine compartment. I cut the curves from solid, leaving sufficient thickness on the front of the chassis members to accommodate the spring hangers. Be sure to drill all the chassis holes before shaping starts.

2. The two main chassis members are held together by three cross pieces. The two members in the middle are stub morticed and tenoned into the chassis. The one cross piece at the back is secured with a halving joint. The chassis decking is made from solid ash as I felt that plywood was not of a sufficiently high standard. The decking has to be planed to thickness and is glued on to the top of the chassis.

3. The springs are made from nickel silver but you don't have to be an engineer to shape them. The curved section of the spring is formed using round nosed pliers. The spring material is easily cut with tin snips. To give a touch of realism the springs are held together by spring clamps that are folded around the leaves. This is not as difficult as it sounds. Once each spring has been made drill the spring fixing holes. The springs are attached to the car with ash spring hangers. The front springs are attached to the chassis fairly easily but the rear mounting of the front springs is a little more complicated. Due to the width of the springs and the curvature of the chassis it is necessary to glue small blocks either side of the chassis to build up the width so that the spring hangers when attached will fit either side of the spring. The back springs are far easier to attach as there are no spring hangers to complicate matters. Attachment to the chassis is by rod and spring clips and at the back by screws fitted with cup washers.

4. Mark out and cut the rear axle to shape. Provision is made on the top for the springs to be attached and a centre hole to take the prop shaft. The stub axles holding the back wheels are glued into the rear axle.

5. The front axle has now to be cut and shaped, on cars of this period the heavy forged section axle was a prominent feature. The stub axles for the wheels are glued in with epoxy resin.

6. The front headlamps are mounted on a bar which runs right through the chassis (very careful work is required here) and on the outer edge the front mudguard supports are fitted. The headlamps are turned on a lathe and 'cradles' made for them to be mounted in. Aluminium rod is used to mount the headlamps on to the support blocks that are held in place by the centre bar running through the chassis. The number plate is glued to the underside of the bar.

7. The engine cylinder block and sump are made in two separate halves. The hole in the block takes the radiator fan. The fan body was turned on a lathe and the blades attached separately. The cranking handle goes into the sump and is held at the front end by a block that is screwed into the underside of the radiator block. Getting wooden dowels to turn in wood smoothly can be achieved if you first find some plastic tube that has the same internal diameter as the dowel rod. This is inserted in the holes and makes a good bearing surface. To get the crank to turn the fan smoothly I used elastic

bands, but it's a delicate piece of work and takes time.

8.   The radiator is now shaped. On to the main shaped block are implanted 2 side strips and a top piece which are all the same thickness as the black plastic grill. The small RR badge is available but limited to just 100. Drill the hole in the top to take the flying lady. The famous statue is made from 2 pieces – a circular plug turned on the lathe into which the feet of the lady are implanted. The shaping of the lady is really a task for very small gouge and if you have them 'rifler files' – the figure shown was my seventh attempt!

The back of the radiator is drilled to take the water pipe from the top of the cylinder block. The water pipes are made from aluminium rod. The radiator is glued between the front chassis members.

9.   4 running board supports are now made and glued on to the chassis. The exhaust silencer (dowel rod) is held to the body work by thin strips of brass. An aluminium tube forms the back pipe while the front pipe is bent to shape from a piece of aluminium rod. Having no rear views of the car I was unable to be sure of the end detailing of the pipe – did it have a large fish tail as did the Bentleys – I wonder?

10.   The running boards have a beautiful sweeping line. I cut mine from the solid using an Inca bandsaw – super accurate. Now there is no real need to cut it all in one piece, you can cut the rear arch separately, but for me it was a challenge to cut it in one piece, and as thin as possible.

Cut out the inside curves first and clean off all the saw marks. Now drill the holes for the front mudguard supports. Obviously with such a thin section of wood, very careful boring of the hole is essential otherwise the mudguard will be spoilt. Once this is completed, cut out the other side and glasspaper off the saw marks. The mudguard is very thin but being made from ash it is still strong and flexible.

The mudguard rear support is a piece of aluminium bar on to which are filed two 'flats'. The flats increase the gluing area when attaching the mudguards to the bar. Epoxy resin glue is essential for this task. The mudguard front support bars are bent from aluminium tube. You will find that aluminium is a very useful alloy as it is so very easy to bend. You will need to do a bit of 'trial and error' – offering up the mudguard to the supports

and bending the aluminium bars until you achieve wings of the same height on both sides.

You will need to make two mudguard support clips. These are screwed into the back of the chassis. The screws used are raised head chrome plated.

11.   The boat-shaped body is now formed. From the main block the passenger compartment is cut. The seat portion is cut out using a variety of chisels and gouges. The engine bulkhead is then glued onto the front section of the compartment. It is very difficult to detail all the shaping that is necessary, however keep placing the body on the chassis and continue working until a gentle flowing line is achieved. Remember these cars were hand made and all the panels hand beaten, so every one would be slightly different – no nasty pre-shaped metal boxes in those days!

The boat-shaped tail is enhanced by the use of Brazilian mahogany which is glued in place and shaped. The dashboard is now cut and fitted as in the steering wheel.

12.   Before you glue the body to the decking it is essential to make the bonnet. Now to give this a realistic feel I cut a small slot (with a tenon saw) length-ways on the top and fitted a piece of brass wire, it looks just like a hinged joint! To make sure that the bonnet locates, small strips of wood are glued on the inside edges of the radiator and bulkhead. When the bonnet is in place these small strips hold everything firm. It is therefore very helpful to have some adjustment when doing all these fittings to achieve a moveable rear section.

The cab is lined with felt on the floor and leather for seats and cab edges. A fine leather is quite easily shaped and held in place using a leather glue.

FITTINGS

There are many turned parts, headlamps, horn trumpets, knobs, side lights, fuel tanks. A lathe will obviously be of tremendous help but good results can be obtained by having an electric drill in a stand, mounting the wood in the chuck and turning the small pieces to shape – not easy, but possible. The brake lever and gear change are situated on the outside. I made the brake system movable by using nylon cord and elastic bands, but is does not work the brakes.

Two spare cans of petrol are fitted to the running boards. A tool box is also fitted on the running board. You will find that you can go on and on adding detail.

Boat-Tailed Sporting Silver Ghost Cutting List

Chassis Longitudinal Member	2 off 511 × 20 × 16mm (20⅛ × ¾ × ⅝in) timber
Chassis Decking	1 off 451 × 89 × 5mm (17¾ × 3½ × 3/16in) timber
Chassis Intermediate Cross Members	2 off 57 × 20 × 16mm (2¼ × ¾ × ⅝in) timber
Chassis Rear Cross Member	1 off 89 × 16 × 12mm (3½ × ⅝ × ½in) timber
Petrol Tank	1 off 89 × 28 × 25mm (3½ × 1⅛ × 1in) timber
Number Plate	1 off 44 × 12 × 3mm (1¾ × ½ × ⅛in) timber
Rear Light	2 off 20mm (¾in) × 12mm (½in) diam dowel
Rear Axle	1 off 140 × 22 × 16mm (5½ × ⅞ × ⅝in) timber
Front Axle	1 off 140 × 41 × 16mm (5½ × 1⅝ × ⅝in) timber
Engine Sump	1 off 127 × 41 × 32mm (5 × 1⅝ × 1¼in) timber
Gear Box	1 off 60 × 35 × 28mm (2⅜ × 1⅜ × 1⅛in) timber
Prop. Shaft	1 off 171mm (6¾in) × 6mm (¼in) diam dowel
Exhaust	1 off 146mm (5¾in) × 16mm (⅝in) diam dowel
Brake Equalizing Rod Assembly	2 off 28 × 9 × 9mm (1⅛ × ⅜ × ⅜in) timber
Brake/Gear Lever Assembly	1 off 35 × 25 × 9mm (1⅜ × 1 × ⅜in) timber
	1 off 28 × 28 × 3mm (1⅛ × 1⅛ × ⅛in) timber
Gear Lever	1 off 102 × 9 × 3mm (4 × ⅜ × ⅛in) timber
Brake Lever	1 off 102 × 9 × 3mm (4 × ⅜ × ⅛in) timber
Mudguard/Running Board	2 off 525 × 84 × 28mm (21 × 3½ × 1⅛in) timber
Running Board Support	4 off 76 × 44 × 6mm (3 × 1¾ × ¼in) timber
Toolbox	1 off 60 × 25 × 25mm (2⅜ × 1 × 1in) timber
Petrol Can	2 off 28 × 25 × 20mm (1⅛ × 1 × ¾in) timber
	Make from 38mm (1½in) × 9mm (⅜in) diam dowel
Side Light	Make from 28mm (1⅛in) × 12mm (½in) diam dowel
	Make from 25mm (1in) × 3mm (⅛in) diam dowel
Body Assembly	1 off 292 × 102 × 51mm (11½ × 4 × 2in) timber
	1 off 102 × 57 × 22mm (4 × 2¼ × ⅞in) timber
	1 off 171 × 102 × 8mm (6¾ × 4 × 5/16in) timber
Body Assembly	2 off 38 × 6 × 3mm (1½ × ¼ × ⅛in) timber
Steering Wheel Assembly	1 off 83mm (3¼in) × 6mm (¼in) diam dowel
	1 off 6mm (¼in) × 35mm (1⅜in) diam dowel
Windscreen Frame	1 off 89 × 39 × 5mm (3½ × 1 9/16 × 3/16in) timber
Dashboard Assembly	1 off 86 × 28 × 1.5mm (3⅜ × 1⅛ × 1/16in) timber
	1 off 102 × 20 × 6mm (4 × ¾ × ¼in) timber
Seat	1 off 83 × 44 × 6mm (3¼ × 1¾ × ¼in) timber
Bonnet	1 off 135 × 67 × 25mm (5 5/16 × 2⅝ × 1in) timber
	2 off 135 × 44 × 6mm (5 5/16 × 1¾ × ¼in) timber
Starting Handle Assembly	1 off 22 × 9 × 9mm (⅞ × ⅜ × ⅜in) timber
	1 off 86mm (3⅜in) × 6mm (¼in) diam dowel
	1 off 28mm (1⅛in) × 6mm (¼in) diam dowel
Pulley	1 off 16mm (⅝in) × 20mm (¾in) diam dowel
Engine	1 off 114 × 32 × 28mm (4½ × 1¼ × 1⅛in) timber
	1 off 114 × 9 × 6mm (4½ × ⅜ × ¼in) timber
Cooling Fan	1 off 16mm (⅝in) × 28mm (1⅛in) diam dowel
Fan Blades	Make from 76 × 5 × 1.5mm (3 × 3/16 × 1/16in) timber
Radiator	1 off 89 × 67 × 20mm (3½ × 2⅝ × ¾in) timber
	1 off 89 × 67 × 3mm (3½ × 2⅝ × ⅛in) timber
	1 off 44 × 12 × 9mm (1¾ × ½ × ⅜in) timber
	1 off 14 × 8 × 1.5mm (9/16 × 5/16 × 1/16in) timber
	2 off 38 × 6 × 3mm (1½ × ¼ × ⅛in) timber
Spotlight/Acetylene Tank Assembly	1 off 25mm (1in) × 28mm (1⅛in) diam dowel
	1 off 41mm (1⅝in) × 20mm (¾in) diam dowel
	1 off 16mm (⅝in) × 12mm (½in) diam dowel
	1 off 28 × 12 × 3mm (1⅛ × ½ × ⅛in) timber
Radiator Emblem	1 off 35 × 21 × 20mm (1⅜ × 13/16 × ¾in) timber

Boat-Tailed Sporting Silver Ghost Cutting List *continued*

Horn	1 off 16mm (5/8in) × 16mm (5/8in) diam dowel
	1 off 12mm (1/2in) × 12mm (1/2in) diam dowel
Headlamp Acetylene Tank	1 off 35mm (13/8in) × 20mm (3/4in) diam dowel
	1 off 12mm (1/2in) × 12mm (1/2in) diam dowel
Headlamp Assembly	2 off 25mm (1in) × 30mm (13/16) diam dowel
	2 off 28 × 12 × 6mm (11/8 × 1/2 × 1/4in) timber
	2 off 22 × 9 × 9mm (7/8 × 3/8 × 3/8in) timber
Front Mudguard Support Mountings	2 off 20 × 9 × 9mm (3/4 × 3/8 × 3/8in) timber
Front Number Plate	1 off 44 × 12 × 3mm (13/4 × 1/2 × 1/8in) timber
Front Spring Assembly Hangers	8 off 28 × 16 × 3mm (11/8 × 5/8 × 1/8in) timber
Front Spring Assembly Rear Attachment Spacer	2 off 12 × 12 × 6mm (1/2 × 1/2 × 1/4in) timber
Front Spring Assembly Rear Attachment Spacer	2 off 12 × 12 × 3mm (1/2 × 1/2 × 1/8in) timber
Headlamp Mounting Bar	1 off 102mm (4in) 6mm (1/4in) diam dowel
Ancillaries	4 off 108mm (41/4in) diam road wheels
	2 off 35mm (13/8in) × 6mm (1/4in) diam steel front stub axles
	2 off 51mm (2in) × 6mm (1/4in) diam steel rear stub axles
	4 off 6mm (1/4in) spring dome caps
	Make from 800 × 16 × 1.5mm (311/2 × 5/8 × 1/16in) spring steel – front springs
	Make from 900 × 16 × 1.5mm (351/2 × 5/8 × 1/16in) spring steel – rear springs
	Make from 400 × 16 × 1.5mm (153/4 × 5/8 × 1/16in) spring steel – clamps
	8 off 28mm (11/8in) × 5mm (3/16in) diam steel rods – front axle spring pins
	16 off 5mm (3/16in) spring dome caps
	2 off 36mm (17/16in) × 5mm (3/16in) diam steel rods – rear axle spring pins (front)
	4 off 5mm (3/16in) spring dome caps
	1 off 111mm (43/8in) × 5mm (3/16in) alloy rod – brake rod assembly
	1 off 127mm (5in) × 6mm (1/4in) alloy rod – exhaust
	1 off 160mm (61/4in) × 9mm (3/8in) o/diam alloy tube – exhaust
	1 off 191mm (71/2in) × 5mm (3/16in) diam alloy rod – mudguard rear support
	2 off 76mm (3in) × 3mm (1/8in) diam alloy rod – mudguard front support
	Make from 254mm (10in) × 6mm (1/4in) thin metal strip for clips
	1 off 11 × 6 × 1.5mm (7/16 × 1/4 × 1/16in) brass – toolbox insert
	1 off 89 × 41 × 1.5mm (31/2 × 15/8 × 1/16in) clear plastic windscreen
	1 off 135mm (55/16in) × 1.5mm (1/16in) diam brass rod – bonnet hinge
	1 off 73 × 60 × 3mm (27/8 × 23/8 × 1/8in) ribbed black plastic – radiator
	Make from 152mm (6in) × 5mm (3/16in) diam alloy rod – engine 'hose'
	1 off 28mm (11/8in) × 5mm (3/16in) diam steel rod – fan shaft
	1 off 152mm (6in) × 3mm (1/8in) diam alloy rod – spot light
	Make from 114mm (41/2in) × 5mm (3/16in) diam alloy rod – headlamp
	1 off 114mm (41/2in) × 3mm (1/8in) diam alloy rod – horn
	1 off 114mm (41/2in) × 3mm (1/8in) diam alloy rod – acetylene tank
	1 off 152mm (6in) × 152mm (6in) soft leather for upholstery

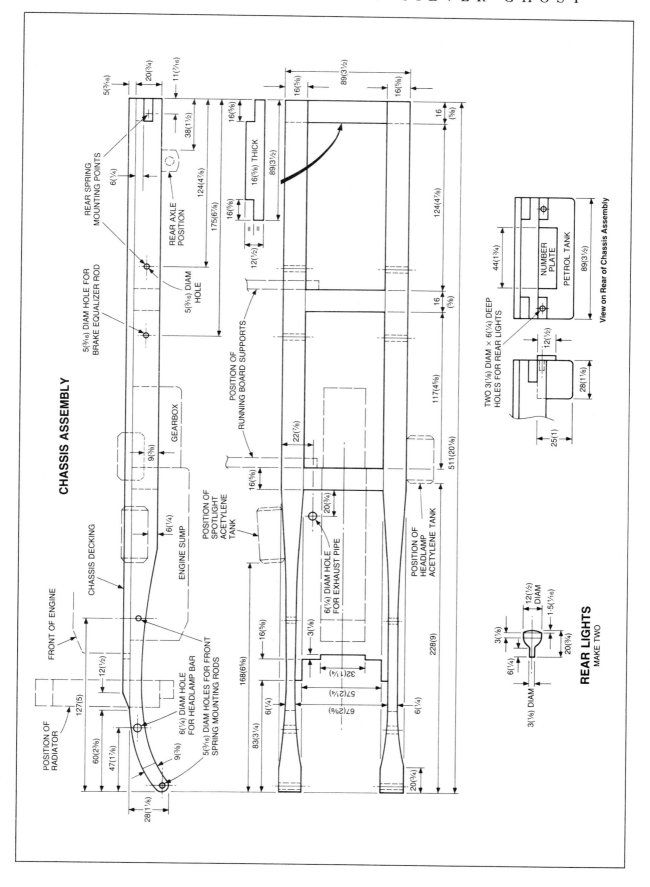

CHASSIS ASSEMBLY

REAR LIGHTS
MAKE TWO

View on Rear of Chassis Assembly

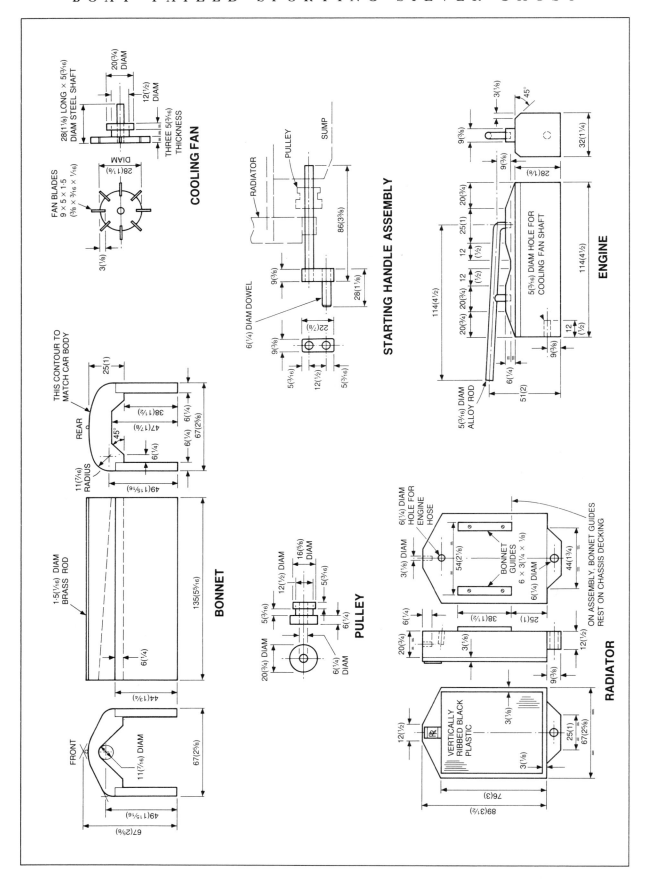

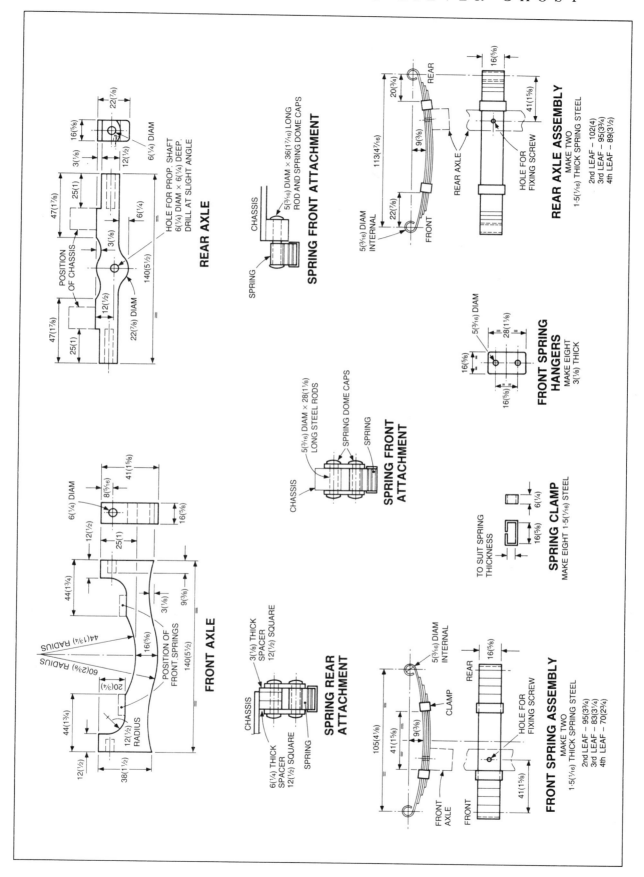

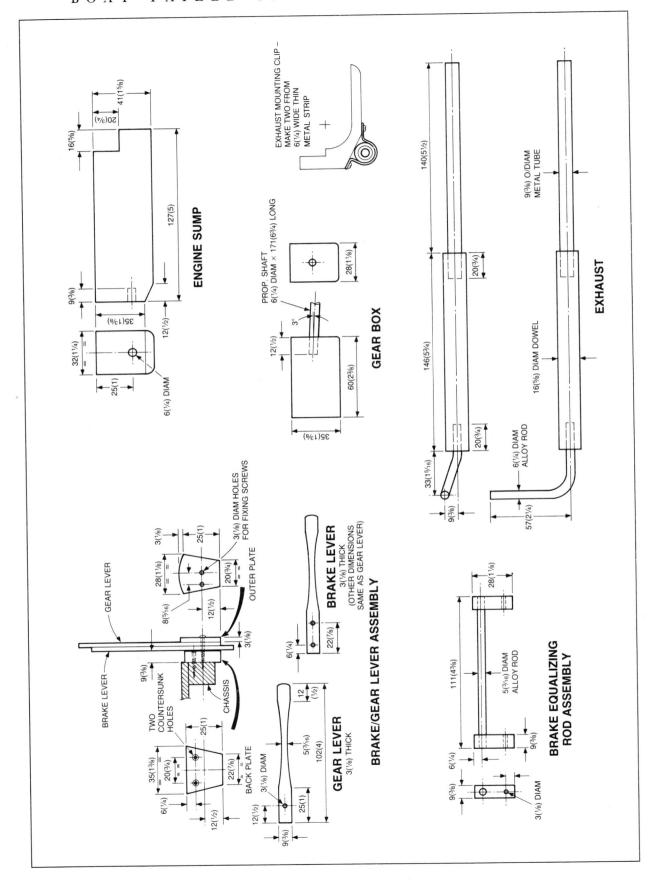

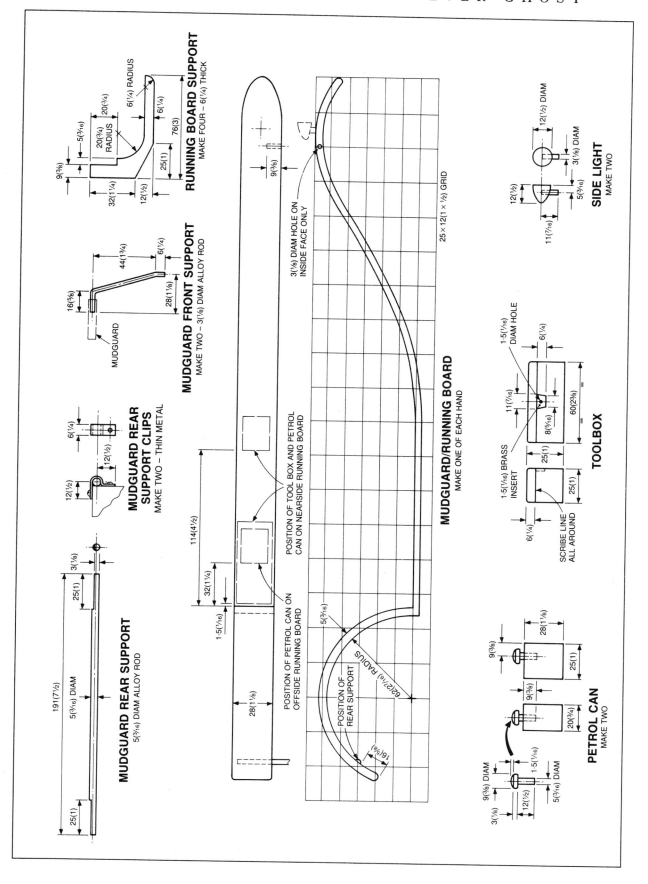

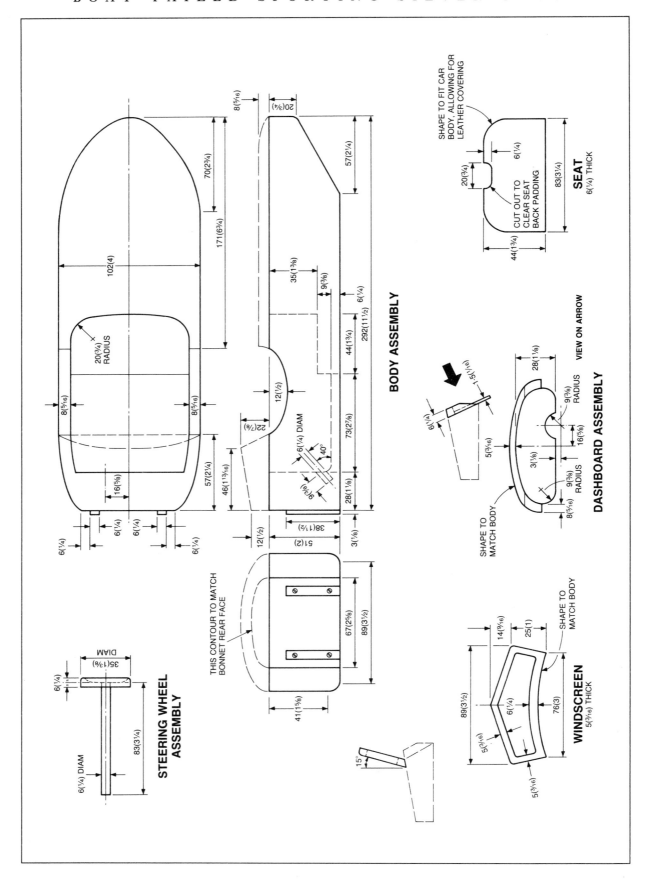

BODY ASSEMBLY

SEAT
6(¼) THICK

DASHBOARD ASSEMBLY

VIEW ON ARROW

WINDSCREEN
5(³/₁₆) THICK

STEERING WHEEL ASSEMBLY

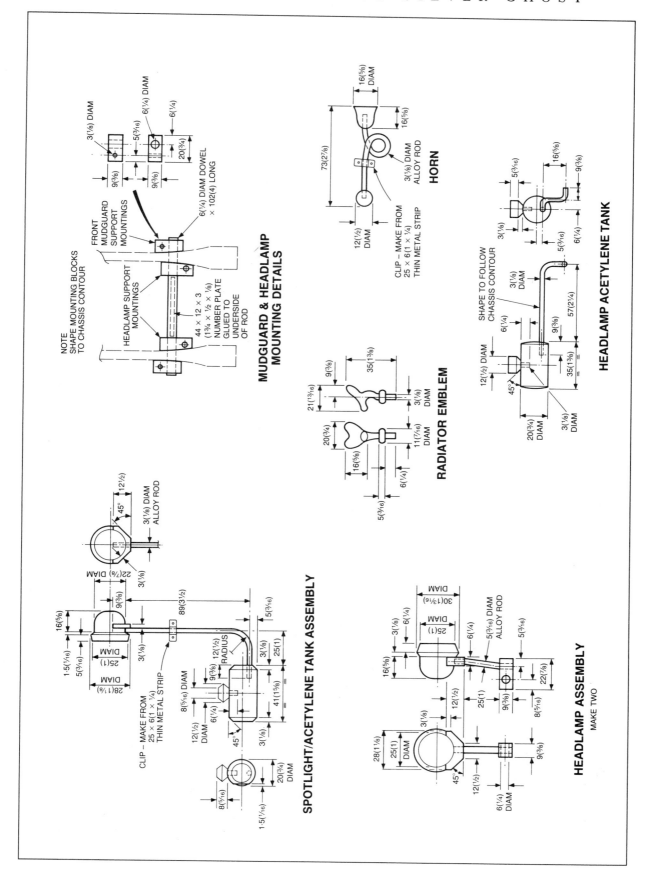

MUDGUARD & HEADLAMP MOUNTING DETAILS

HORN

RADIATOR EMBLEM

HEADLAMP ACETYLENE TANK

SPOTLIGHT/ACETYLENE TANK ASSEMBLY

HEADLAMP ASSEMBLY
MAKE TWO

FIRE ENGINE

(See colour plate 16)

I have always had a fascination for fire engines and I suppose it was inevitable that my visit to America should result in actually seeing one of these enormous rescue machines in New York. Ward Le France is a very old and famous fire engine maker and it is from this stable that this gigantic machine comes.

Before building any toy or model there are always things to be taken into consideration. Before you start this model perhaps it would be best to find a place where you are going to park it, and sufficient room to extend the ladders that reach almost 8 feet! If your house is fitted with a water meter, this engine is fitted with 4 pumps and 2 reservoirs – so your consumption of water is bound to increase!

Once you have overcome all the logistic problems, it's a great engine to build and will undoubtedly make you popular with the children!

TIMBER

All the mainframes, chassis, ladders etc. are made in Nordic redwood and 'trimmed' with Brazilian mahogany.

TO MAKE

1. A start is made by marking out the chassis for the tractor unit (tractor is a name universally used for the part of an articulated vehicle that has the propulsion unit). Drill the front and back axle holes. To mount the trailer unit parallel it is necessary to glue three blocks together and fit them onto the back of the chassis. The blocks are secured to the chassis by screwing from the underside.

2. Mark out a pair of cab sides and cut out the wheel arches carefully. The side screens are glued onto the cab sides. Cut out the windows and remove all the saw cuts. The side screen is then glued onto the cab side.

The cab front panel is now shaped. Spend time in getting a nice smooth curve and then make the radiator grille. Edging strips are glued around the outside of the grille and the centre is fitted with a piece of aluminium mesh.

The headlamps are cut from a piece of orange reflector (the sort used in car door buffer guards).

3. The windscreen is now shaped and a piece of perspex prepared. Don't cut the perspex to size until the cab has been glued up. Make the steering wheel and dashboard and leave final assembly until the sides are glued together.

4. Mark out and cut the water compartment sides. The sides fit behind the cab sides and 'blank off' the wheel arch. The compartment sides also form the fixing position for the front seat.

The twin water pumps are mounted on the back of the compartment. The water container is made from an 'adapted' lunch box, a large hole being bored in the lid to allow the container to be easily refilled, and to hold the pipes that supply the pumps.

5. Assemble the cab 'dry' (without glue) and make sure all the parts fit well. Once you are satisfied, glue the cab and chassis units together.

6. The running boards, doors, wheel arch trims etc. are now shaped up and glued on. I have used a Brazilian mahogany, but the important factor is to use a contrasting colour.

7. The door mirrors are now made and fitted as is the length of flexible plastic-covered curtain wire that acts as the radio mast. Do put a large knob or wooden block on the top for safety – glue it on with epoxy resin glue. Trim the perspex windscreen and secure it with round head chrome plated screws.

8. The axles are cut to length and 'packed out' from the chassis by pieces of rubber tube. Don't fit the wheels until you have varnished the model.

9. The pumps are fitted onto the top of the water container compartment. The hoses run from the water container to the pump and then out of the compartment through the twin pre-drilled holes. When the hoses need to be coupled to the trailer unit, pieces of aluminium tube are used as jointers. It's vital to fit joints otherwise the tractor cannot be disconnected from the trailer.

THE TRAILER

The trailer can be broken into three main components
a) the trailer
b) the turntable
c) the ladders

a) Studying the drawings you can see that this part consists basically of one central spar of timber, at the front of which is a turntable and at the back of which is a boxed bogie wheel arrangement. Two strips of wood (running boards) are fixed either side along the bottom, and onto them the jacks and pump nozzles are mounted.

Having marked and cut to length the central spar timber, cut out the front bulkhead and the turntable platform. Drill a coach bolt in the platform and then glue the bulkhead and platform to the central spar.

Now cut the bulkheads a, b, and c to fit at the back. Bulkhead c is different from a and b and does not require the central spar cut out. Glue the bulkheads onto the central spar adding the top and side panels. Cut out the wheel fairings and glue them into position.

Cut to length the two running boards and glue them onto the bulkheads. Now fit the rear water compartment. The lids on these sandwich boxes are retained, a large hole being drilled in one corner to allow re-fuelling, and smaller holes drilled to take the hoses.

The four hose nozzles are mounted in a tray underneath the main spar. Hoses drilled in the bottom of this tray allow easy access for threading the hoses. The nozzles themselves are housed in holes attached to short lengths of hose. To provide stability swivel jacks are fitted under the running boards. At the far ends, dowel rods act as jacks to level things up.

As the turntable unit is very heavy, the platform holding it needs to be given support. Two shaped pieces of wood are glued onto the underside of the turntable and to the sides of the front bulkhead. This wooden 'bracket' gives additional strength.

The main spar is fitted with a hefty dowel rod that locates in the hole drilled in the tractor chassis.

b) The turntable consists of four main pieces, a circular disc onto which a square piece of timber is mounted which in turn has two side pieces that hold all the winding handles etc.

Make a start by drilling the hole to take the coach bolt. Now cut out the circular disc. A good dark pencil line is essential, as is a steady hand. The two side pieces that take the handles are now cut and shaped up as a pair. Drill the three holes in the sides, but be sure to keep both pieces fixed together so as to ensure that the ladder winding mechanism works smoothly. Once the holes are drilled, fit offcuts of dowel rod in the holes and attach them to the square base with screws. The screws are put in from the underside. Make sure that the offcuts of dowel rod continue to turn smoothly throughout the fixing operation.

The winding handles are square blocks of wood which have four holes drilled in them to take dowel rods. This arrangement makes excellent winding handles. Cut out a good stout ratchet arm and ratchet wheel.

The rubber-tyred wheel has to be grooved out in the middle. There are many ways of doing this, the most primitive probably being to mount the wheel onto a bolt that is in turn fitted onto the chuck of an electric drill. With the drill firmly fixed in a stand, use a file to remove the rubber in the middle of the tyre – but be careful.

When the ladder has been made, 2 springs are used to help counterbalance and raise the ladders.

c) One of the great challenges of making this engine was to get all three ladders telescoping out evenly. You will need to study the 'rigging' diagram very carefully. One essential factor is that the rubber-tyred wheel needs a groove cut in it around which the cord is wound twice. The nylon cord on the bottom ladder is simply a loop that moves the middle ladder up or down. Tied to the top rung of the bottom ladder is the second loop which is threaded beneath the bottom rung of the middle ladder (not tied) and then tied to the bottom rung of the top ladder and then looped over the top rung of the middle ladder, the end being then tied off at the point where it started. It's not as difficult as it sounds but it does rely on you making the ladders run smoothly within each other. The method for making one ladder is the same for all three and does ensure that all the rungs fit.

Select a pair of straight-grained pieces – no knots anywhere along the entire length. Tape the two lengths together and carefully mark the positions for all the rungs (dowel rods). Now drill the holes. The dowel rods must all be cut to exactly the same length. To achieve this make a small jig which will alleviate any inaccuracies of individually measured dowels. Remove the tape and carefully countersink all the holes, which will make it far easier to fit the dowels. A spot of glue is placed on every dowel rod and then with a light hammer a dowel is tapped into each hole. Glue is now applied to the other ends of the dowel rods and the other side fitted. Once the second side is fitted, and all the dowel rods are started in the holes, place the ladder in the vice and, working from one end to the other, tighten the vice jaws on the ladder sides. The dowel rods will be forced into the holes and, because the holes are drilled right through, the dowel rods will eventually touch the vice jaws. This method of construction and assembly ensures that the ladder sides run parallel over its entire length.

Construct all three ladders in exactly the same way. Once the glue is dry, fit the ladders together. It will be necessary to remove dried glue etc. with a sharp plane. Fit the three ladders together and make sure that they slide smoothly.

The ladders are held in place as they slide by ladder guides. These are made by rebating a length of timber and then cutting off four pieces and screwing them onto the ladder sides.

Before any rigging takes place you should varnish the ladders and then apply a good wax polish. Work the polish well into the grain, and fit the ladders together. The ladders should all run smoothly without any snatching. If you have tight spots, take the ladders appart and the tight spot will show clearly as a shiny area on the wood.

Now assemble the ladders in the turntable, fitting the winding handles, springs etc. Rig the ladder as described and, after some initial adjustments, all ladders will elevate evenly – a beautiful sight after all the work and well worth the effort.

STEERING REAR BOGIE

The real machine has such a long trailer that a steering rear bogie is provided. It is operated by a crew member who sits at the back of the trailer. Make the seat, steering etc. and glue them onto the rear steering platform.

LADDER CAGE

Besides the three main elevating ladders these incredible machines have more ladders stored in the ladder cage. Mark out and cut the material for the cage. The four longitudinal pieces are held together top and bottom by eight vertical posts, and the two units joined by dowel rods.

Bottom spacers are then glued onto the cage and these in turn are screwed to the main spar of the trailer. The ladders are all made by the method already described (see above) and fit into the cage. To prevent them all spilling out, ladder pegs are made which lock them all in place.

The rear steering platform is now screwed onto the back of the ladder cage.

WATER HOSES AND PUMPS

These are best fitted following the diagram. There is no limit to the number of pumps you can fit, but four does seem a good number for such a prestigious machine.

The diagram only shows 2 pumps – back and front. The other side is arranged in exactly the same way. I found the use of electric cable clips very helpful when fixing the tubing to the wood and trying to get tidy pipe runs. The nails in these clips are exchanged for screws.

It is essential to get the non-return valves fitted in the right direction – double check this. The pumps will not work properly until they are primed (full of water). Once water is in all the tubes and the valves of the pumps they will work efficiently.

Fire Engine Cutting List

Chassis	1 off 555 × 197 × 20mm (21 7/8 × 7 3/4 × 3/4in) timber
	1 off 215 × 25 × 9mm (8 1/2 × 1 × 3/8in) timber
	2 off 92 × 20 × 9mm (3 5/8 × 3/4 × 3/8in) timber
	2 off 203 × 20 × 9mm (8 × 3/4 × 3/8in) timber
	1 off 197 × 76 × 20mm (7 3/4 × 3 × 3/4in) timber
	2 off 152 × 76 × 20mm (6 × 3 × 3/4in) timber
Cab Side	2 off 203 × 171 × 12mm (8 × 6 3/4 × 1/2in) timber
	2 off 79 × 9 × 9mm (3 1/8 × 3/8 × 3/8in) timber
	2 off 130 × 85 × 9mm (5 1/8 × 3 5/16 × 3/8in) timber
Mirror	2 off 38 × 20 × 6mm (1 1/2 × 3/4 × 1/4in) timber
Water Compartment and Seat	2 off 322 × 102 × 12mm (12 5/8 × 4 × 1/2in) timber
	2 off 178 × 12 × 9mm (7 × 1/2 × 3/8in) timber
	1 off 171 × 83 × 12mm (6 3/4 × 3 1/4 × 1/2in) timber
	1 off 146 × 102 × 12mm (5 3/4 × 4 × 1/2in) timber
	1 off 171 × 51 × 12mm (6 3/4 × 2 × 1/2in) timber
	1 off 171 × 35 × 12mm (6 3/4 × 1 3/8 × 1/2in) timber
	1 off 171 × 140 × 12mm (6 3/4 × 5 1/2 × 1/2in) timber
Windscreen	1 off 197 × 92 × 12mm (7 3/4 × 3 5/8 × 1/2in) timber
Radiator Grille and Headlamps	1 off 178 × 57 × 9mm (7 × 2 1/4 × 3/8in) timber
	2 off 25 × 16 × 3mm (1 × 5/8 × 1/8in) timber
	2 off 114 × 6 × 1.5mm (4 1/2 × 1/4 × 1/16in) timber
	2 off 40 × 5 × 1.5mm (1 9/16 × 3/16 × 1/16in) timber
Cab Front Panel	1 off 197 × 102 × 20mm (7 3/4 × 4 × 3/4in) timber
Dashboard	1 off 165 × 30 × 11mm (6 1/2 × 1 3/16 × 7/16in) timber
Steering Wheel	1 off 6mm (1/4in) × 32mm (1 1/4in) diam dowel
Steering Column	1 off 38mm (1 1/2in) × 6mm (1/4in) diam dowel
Trailer Main Spar	1 off 1118 × 76 × 20mm (44 × 3 × 3/4in) timber
Trailer Front Platform	1 off 223 × 191 × 20mm (8 3/4 × 7 1/2 × 3/4in) timber
Front Bulkhead	1 off 223 × 95 × 20mm (8 3/4 × 3 3/4 × 3/4in) timber
Fillets	2 off 171 × 95 × 20mm (6 3/4 × 3 3/4 × 3/4in) timber
Hitch Pin	1 off 64mm (2 1/2in) × 16mm (5/8in) diam dowel
Pump Mounting Strip	1 off 203 × 57 × 12mm (8 × 2 1/4 × 1/2in) timber
Hose Carrier	1 off 184 × 102 × 20mm (7 1/4 × 4 × 3/4in) timber
	2 off 102 × 32 × 20mm (4 × 1 1/4 × 3/4in) timber

Fire Engine Cutting List *continued*

Running Board	2 off 711 × 32 × 20mm (28 × 1¼ × ¾in) timber
Top Panel	1 off 254 × 59 × 12mm (10 × 2 5/16 × ½in) timber
Rear Bulkheads	3 off 194 × 76 × 20mm (7⅝ × 3 × ¾in) timber
Side Panel	2 off 57 × 57 × 20mm (2¼ × 2¼ × ¾in) timber
Wheel Fairing	2 off 178 × 70 × 8mm (7 × 2¾ × 5/16in) timber
Rear Running Board	2 off 95 × 32 × 20mm (3¾ × 1¼ × ¾in) timber
Rear Axle Block	1 off 178 × 76 × 20mm (7 × 3 × ¾in) timber
Rear Water Container Platform	1 off 191 × 89 × 9mm (7½ × 3½ × ⅜in) timber
	1 off 159 × 28 × 6mm (6¼ × 1⅛ × ¼in) timber
Rear Steering Platform	1 off 191 × 178 × 12mm (7½ × 7 × ½in) timber
	2 off 52mm (2in) × 9mm (⅜in) diam dowel
	1 off 111 × 102 × 12mm (4⅜ × 4 × ½in) timber
	1 off 102 × 70 × 11mm (4 × 2¾ × 7/16in) timber
Dashboard	1 off 70 × 25 × 11mm (2¾ × 1 × 7/16in) timber
Steering Wheel	1 off 9mm (⅜in) × 32mm (1¼in) diam dowel
Steering Column	1 off 36mm (1 7/16in) × 6mm (¼in) diam dowel
Seat	1 off 70 × 38 × 34mm (2¾ × 1½ × 1⅜in) timber
Ladder Cage	4 off 921 × 20 × 20mm (36¼ × ¾ × ¾in) timber
Bottom Spacers	4 off 194 × 35 × 20mm (7⅝ × 1⅜ × ¾in) timber
Side Vertical Posts	10 off 92 × 20 × 20mm (3⅝ × ¾ × ¾in) timber
Top Spacers	10 off 194mm (7⅝in) × 9mm (⅜in) diam dowel
Rear Tie Bar	2 off 178 × 20 × 20mm (7 × ¾ × ¾in) timber
Removeable Ladders	12 off 940 × 20 × 8mm (37 × ¾ × 5/16in) timber
	144 off 38mm (1½in) × 6mm (¼in) diam dowel
Ladder Pegs	4 off 137 × 25 × 20mm (5⅜ × 1. × ¾in) timber
Top Ladder	2 off 1000 × 25 × 6mm (39½ × 1 × ¼in) timber
	26 off 35mm (1⅜in) × 6mm (¼in) diam dowel
Middle Ladder	2 off 1000 × 28 × 8mm (39½ × 1⅛ × 5/16in) timber
	22 off 54mm (2⅛in) × 9mm (⅜in) diam dowel
Bottom Ladder	2 off 1111 × 38 × 11mm (43¾ × 1½ × 7/16in) timber
	20 off 79mm (3⅛in) × 9mm (⅜in) diam dowel
Top Ladder Guide	1 off 83 × 21 × 16mm (3¼ × 13/16 × ⅝in) timber
Middle Ladder Guide	1 off 83 × 21 × 16mm (3¼ × 13/16 × ⅝in) timber
Turntable	1 off 184 × 184 × 20mm (7¼ × 7¼ × ¾in) timber
	1 off 152 × 123 × 20mm (6 × 4¾ × ¾in) timber
	2 off 152 × 85 × 20mm (6 × 3⅜ × ¾in) timber
Ladder Elevating Shaft	1 off 181mm (7⅛in) × 12mm (½in) diam dowel
Winding Handle	3 off 38 × 38 × 20mm (1½ × 1½ × ¾in) timber
	12 off 40mm (1⅝in) × 9mm (⅜in) diam dowel
Ratchet Wheel	1 off 38 × 38 × 20mm (1½ × 1½ × ¾in) timber
Ratchet Arm	1 off 101 × 22 × 20mm (4 × ⅞ × ¾in) timber
Ladder Extending Shaft	1 off 223mm (8¾in) × 12mm (½in) diam dowel
Stabiliser Leg	2 off 508 × 32 × 20mm (20 × 1¼ × ¾in) timber
Foot Retaining Peg	2 off 64mm (2½in) × 6mm (¼in) diam dowel
	2 off 25mm (1in) × 16mm (⅝in) diam dowel
Stabiliser Foot	2 off 67mm (2⅝in) × 6mm (¼in) diam dowel
Ancillaries	10 off 102mm (4in) diam road wheels
	2 off 235mm (9¼in) × 6mm (¼in) diam steel front axles
	1 off 228mm (9in) × 6mm (¼in) diam steel rear axle
	6 off 12mm (½in) × 6mm (¼in) /diam hard plastic spacers
	6 off 6mm (¼in) spring dome caps
	2 off 108mm (4¼in) × 1.5mm (1/16in) diam wire mirror arms
	1 off 171 × 89 × 1.5mm (6¾ × 3½ × 1/16in) clear plastic
	1 off 104mm (4⅛in) × 40mm (1 9/16 in) wire mesh
	1 off 89mm (3½in) × 9mm (⅜in) diam coach bolt
	1 off 152mm (6in) × 5mm (3/16in) diam steel pin

Fire Engine Cutting List *continued*

2 off 5mm (³⁄₁₆in) spring dome caps
1 off 6mm (¹⁄₄in) × 12mm (¹⁄₂in) V_{diam} spacer
2 off 32mm (1¹⁄₄in) × 12mm (¹⁄₂in) V_{diam} spacer
1 off 51mm (2in) diam grooved rubber tyred wheel
2 off Water pumps
4 off Non return valves
2 off Nozzles
1 off Hose connector
2 off Water containers
1 off 4 metre (160in) length of hose
1 off 5 metre (200in) length of nylon cord
2 off Tension springs 51mm (2in) centres solid length ×
   9mm (³⁄₈in) diam

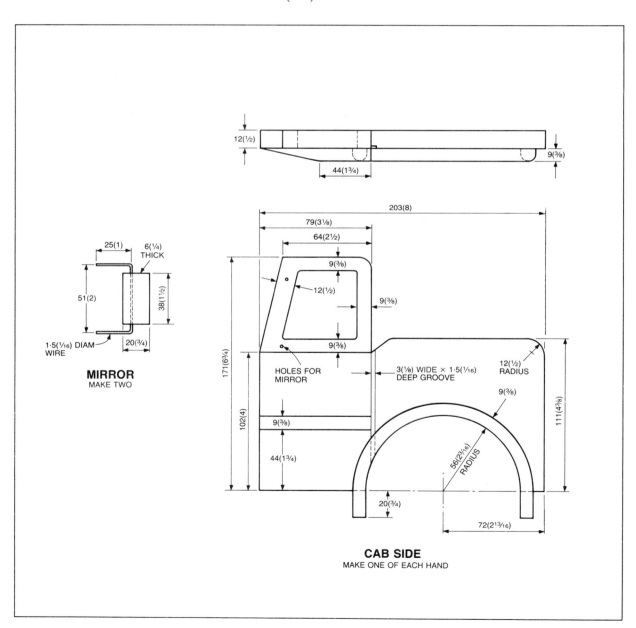

MIRROR
MAKE TWO

CAB SIDE
MAKE ONE OF EACH HAND

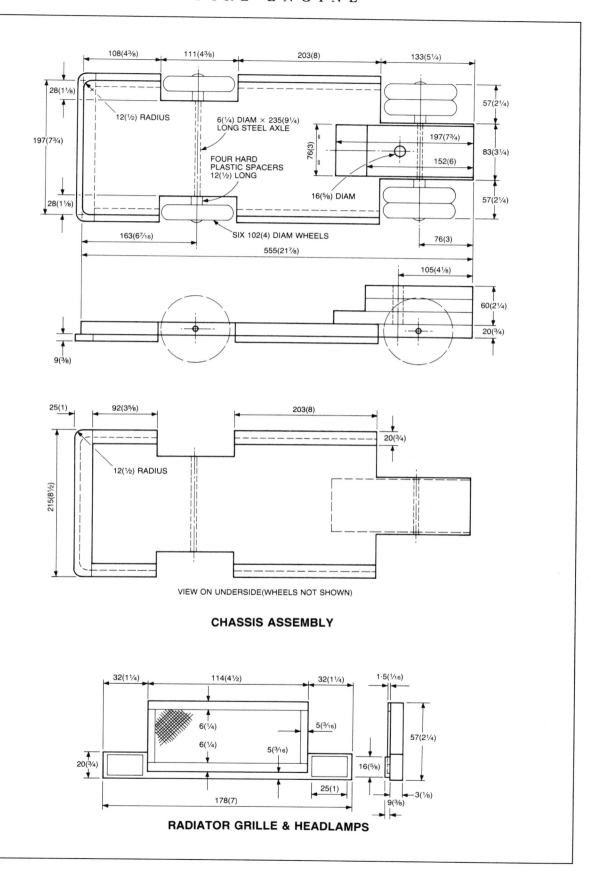

CHASSIS ASSEMBLY

VIEW ON UNDERSIDE(WHEELS NOT SHOWN)

RADIATOR GRILLE & HEADLAMPS

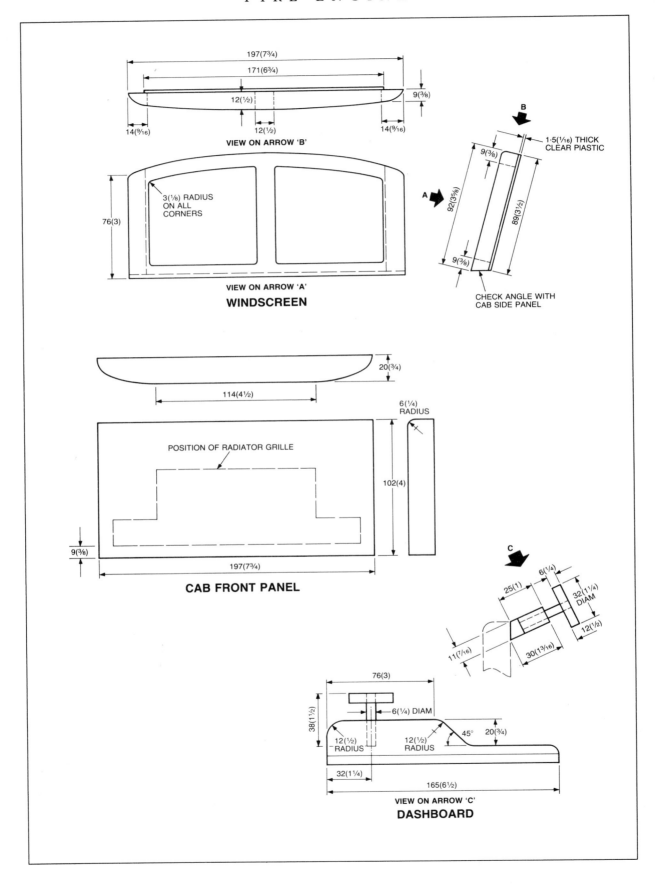

VIEW ON ARROW 'B'

VIEW ON ARROW 'A'
WINDSCREEN

3(⅛) RADIUS
ON ALL
CORNERS

1·5(1/16) THICK
CLEAR PLASTIC

CHECK ANGLE WITH
CAB SIDE PANEL

POSITION OF RADIATOR GRILLE

6(¼)
RADIUS

CAB FRONT PANEL

6(¼) DIAM

12(½)
RADIUS

12(½)
RADIUS

45°

VIEW ON ARROW 'C'
DASHBOARD

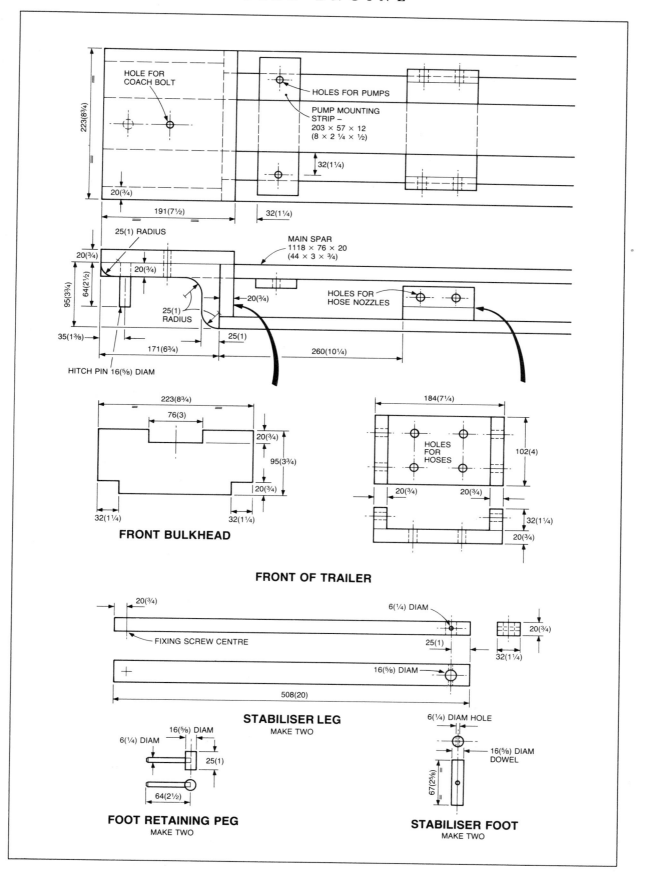

HOLE FOR COACH BOLT

HOLES FOR PUMPS

PUMP MOUNTING STRIP –
203 × 57 × 12
(8 × 2 ¼ × ½)

223(8¾)

20(¾)

191(7½)

32(1¼)

32(1¼)

25(1) RADIUS

MAIN SPAR
1118 × 76 × 20
(44 × 3 × ¾)

20(¾)

20(¾)

95(3¾)

64(2½)

20(¾)

25(1) RADIUS

HOLES FOR HOSE NOZZLES

35(1⅜)

171(6¾)

25(1)

260(10¼)

HITCH PIN 16(⅝) DIAM

223(8¾)

76(3)

20(¾)

95(3¾)

20(¾)

32(1¼)

32(1¼)

FRONT BULKHEAD

184(7¼)

HOLES FOR HOSES

102(4)

20(¾)

20(¾)

32(1¼)

20(¾)

FRONT OF TRAILER

20(¾)

6(¼) DIAM

20(¾)

FIXING SCREW CENTRE

25(1)

32(1¼)

16(⅝) DIAM

508(20)

STABILISER LEG
MAKE TWO

16(⅝) DIAM

6(¼) DIAM

25(1)

64(2½)

FOOT RETAINING PEG
MAKE TWO

6(¼) DIAM HOLE

16(⅝) DIAM DOWEL

67(2⅝)

STABILISER FOOT
MAKE TWO

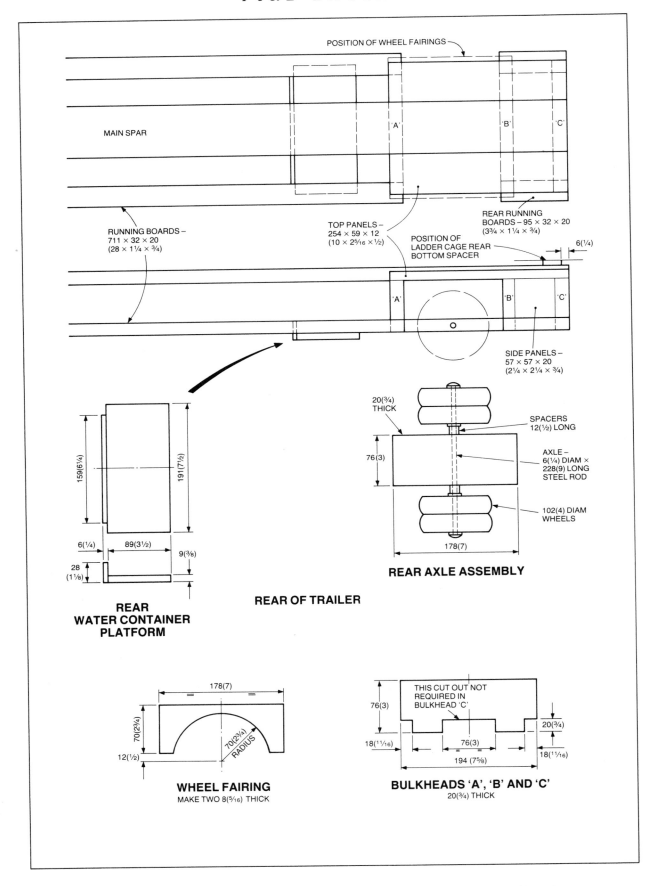

POSITION OF WHEEL FAIRINGS

MAIN SPAR

'A' 'B' 'C'

RUNNING BOARDS –
711 × 32 × 20
(28 × 1¼ × ¾)

TOP PANELS –
254 × 59 × 12
(10 × 2⁵⁄₁₆ × ½)

REAR RUNNING
BOARDS – 95 × 32 × 20
(3¾ × 1¼ × ¾)

POSITION OF
LADDER CAGE REAR
BOTTOM SPACER

6(¼)

'A' 'B' 'C'

SIDE PANELS –
57 × 57 × 20
(2¼ × 2¼ × ¾)

159(6¼)   191(7½)

6(¼)   89(3½)   9(⅜)

28
(1⅛)

**REAR
WATER CONTAINER
PLATFORM**

REAR OF TRAILER

20(¾)
THICK

SPACERS
12(½) LONG

76(3)

AXLE –
6(¼) DIAM ×
228(9) LONG
STEEL ROD

102(4) DIAM
WHEELS

178(7)

REAR AXLE ASSEMBLY

178(7)

70(2¾)

70(2¾)
RADIUS

12(½)

WHEEL FAIRING
MAKE TWO 8(⁵⁄₁₆) THICK

THIS CUT OUT NOT
REQUIRED IN
BULKHEAD 'C'

76(3)

20(¾)

18(¹¹⁄₁₆)   76(3)   18(¹¹⁄₁₆)

194 (7⅝)

BULKHEADS 'A', 'B' AND 'C'
20(¾) THICK

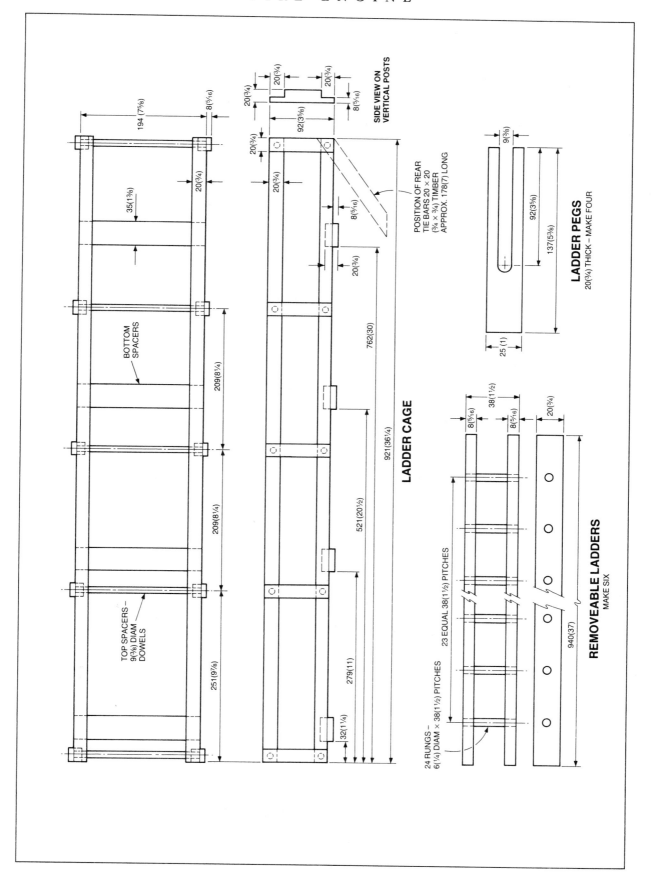

LADDER CAGE

SIDE VIEW ON VERTICAL POSTS

POSITION OF REAR TIE BARS 20 × 20 (³⁄₄ × ³⁄₄) TIMBER APPROX. 178(7) LONG

BOTTOM SPACERS

TOP SPACERS – 9(³⁄₈) DIAM DOWELS

LADDER PEGS
20(³⁄₄) THICK – MAKE FOUR

REMOVEABLE LADDERS
MAKE SIX

23 EQUAL 38(1½) PITCHES

24 RUNGS – 6(¼) DIAM × 38(1½) PITCHES

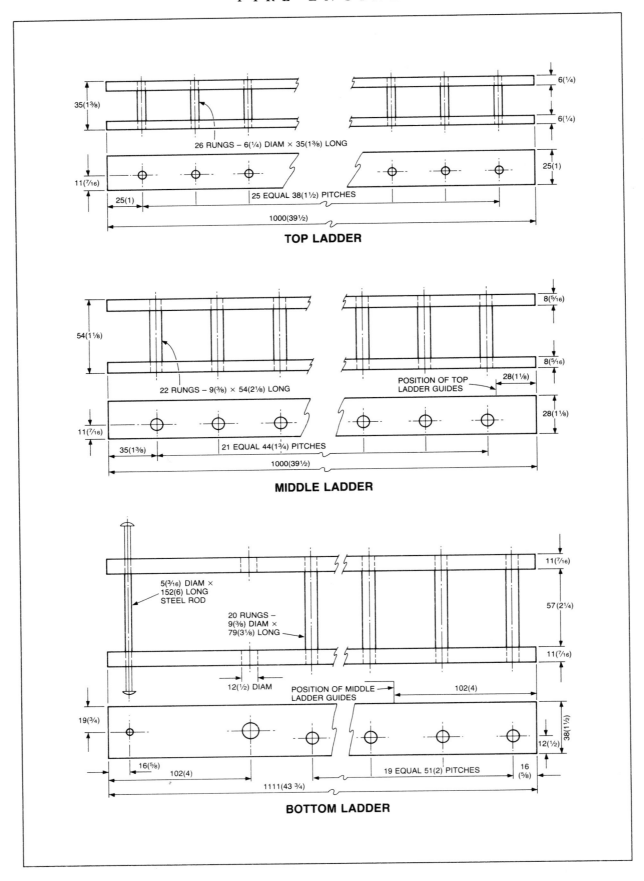

TOP LADDER

MIDDLE LADDER

BOTTOM LADDER

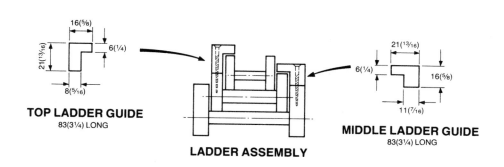

TOP LADDER GUIDE
83(3¼) LONG

LADDER ASSEMBLY

MIDDLE LADDER GUIDE
83(3¼) LONG

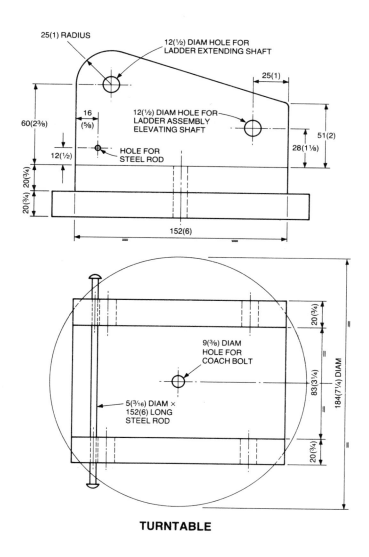

25(1) RADIUS

12(½) DIAM HOLE FOR
LADDER EXTENDING SHAFT

12(½) DIAM HOLE FOR
LADDER ASSEMBLY
ELEVATING SHAFT

25(1)

16
(⅝)

60(2⅜)

51(2)

28(1⅛)

12(½)

HOLE FOR
STEEL ROD

20(¾)

20(¾)

152(6)

9(⅜) DIAM
HOLE FOR
COACH BOLT

5(³⁄₁₆) DIAM ×
152(6) LONG
STEEL ROD

20(¾)

83(3¼)

184(7¼) DIAM

20(¾)

TURNTABLE

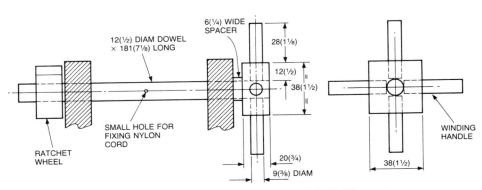

12(½) DIAM DOWEL
× 181(7⅛) LONG

6(¼) WIDE
SPACER

28(1⅛)

12(½)

38(1½)

SMALL HOLE FOR
FIXING NYLON
CORD

RATCHET
WHEEL

20(¾)

9(⅜) DIAM

WINDING
HANDLE

38(1½)

LADDER ASSEMBLY ELEVATING SHAFT

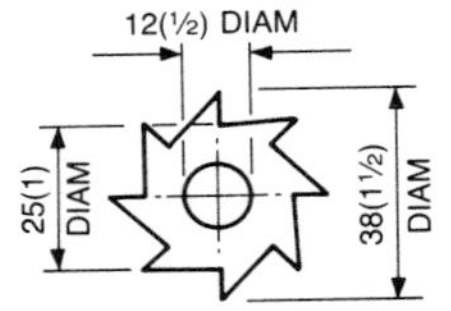

12(½) DIAM

25(1) DIAM

38(1½) DIAM

RATCHET WHEEL
20(¾) THICK

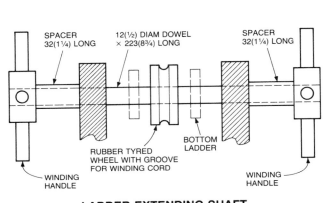

SPACER
32(1¼) LONG

12(½) DIAM DOWEL
× 223(8¾) LONG

SPACER
32(1¼) LONG

RUBBER TYRED
WHEEL WITH GROOVE
FOR WINDING CORD

BOTTOM
LADDER

WINDING
HANDLE

WINDING
HANDLE

LADDER EXTENDING SHAFT

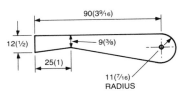

90(3⁹⁄₁₆)

12(½)

9(⅜)

25(1)

11(⁷⁄₁₆)
RADIUS

RATCHET ARM
20(¾) THICK

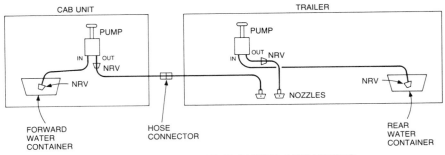

CAB UNIT

PUMP

IN   OUT

NRV

NRV

TRAILER

PUMP

IN   OUT   NRV

NOZZLES

NRV

FORWARD
WATER
CONTAINER

HOSE
CONNECTOR

REAR
WATER
CONTAINER

ARRANGEMENT OF WATER PUMPS AND HOSES
TWO SYSTEMS REQUIRED USING COMMON WATER CONTAINERS
NRV = NON RETURN VALVE

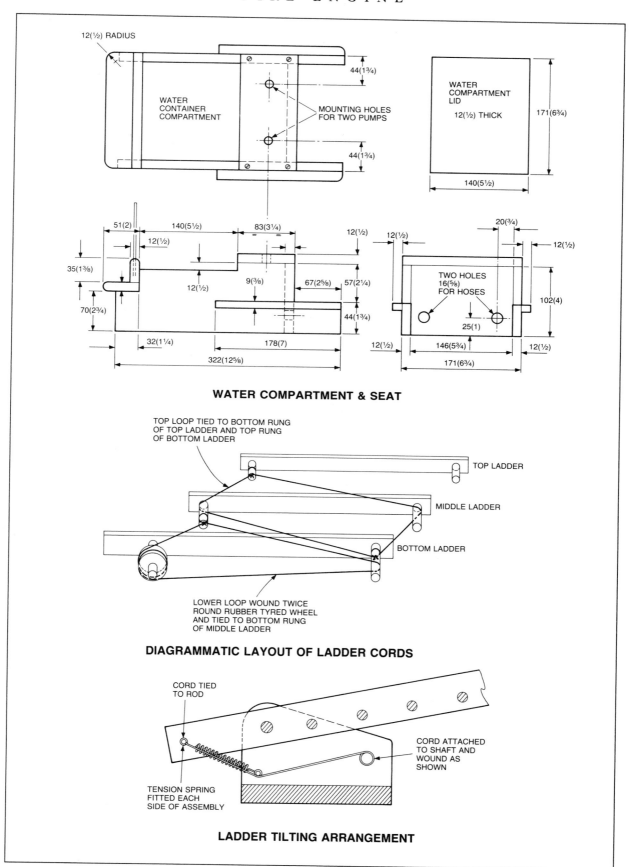

WATER COMPARTMENT & SEAT

DIAGRAMMATIC LAYOUT OF LADDER CORDS

LADDER TILTING ARRANGEMENT

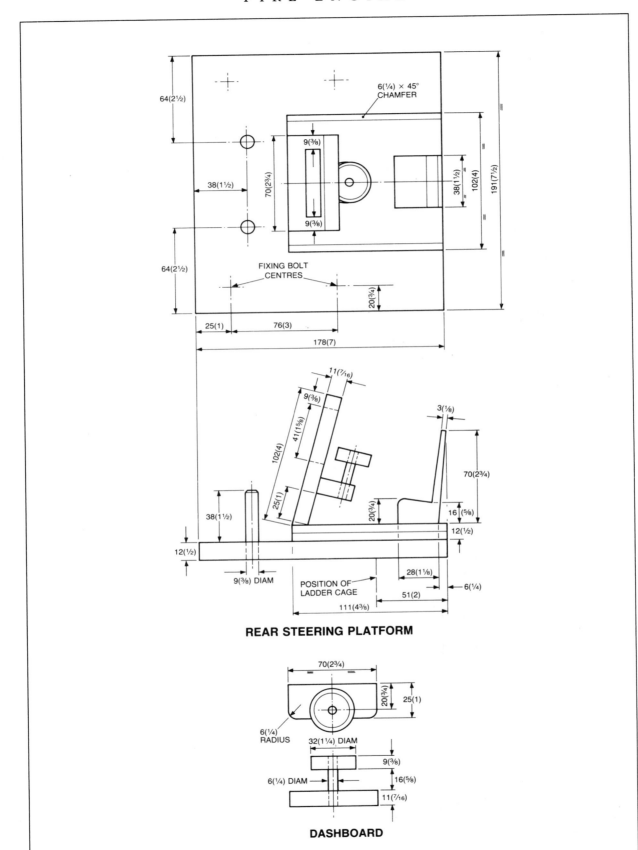

REAR STEERING PLATFORM

DASHBOARD

M A N 6-WHEEL TIPPER TRUCK

(See colour plate 17)

Whenever I pass a construction site I am always interested to discover what equipment they are using. The yellow Volvo articulated dump truck plying to and fro, the JCB's digging endless miles of track – they always look such 'happy' machines in their bright yellow livery. However it's not long before one of my favourite workhorses turns up, the six-wheel tipper waggon. These machines are really the 'Jacks of all trades' they have to be agile to work on 'A' roads hauling rock, gravel etc. but also have to be sufficiently sturdy to work on in clay and mud. A machine that has a dual role has to be to a very high specification as an all rounder, otherwise it will not last very long.

TIMBER
The model is built from Finnish Redwood and although the majority of pieces are stock size some planing will be necessary for a limited number of parts.

TO MAKE
1. The chassis has to be made first, so select two lengths of knot-free timber and tape them together. Now mark out the axle positions and the slots that take the bearers for the tipper bed. With both sides firmly together cut out the slots for the bearers and drill the axle holes. The axle hole in the centre should be a little larger than the rest – ideally a vertical slot to allow the rear bogie to articulate slightly. Now shape up the front of the chassis. The chassis sides are held together by a bumper at the front, two cross members beneath the cab, one member just behind the front wheels and a bar at the back that runs the full width of the chassis.

The front bumper is the only piece that requires some shaping, so start by marking out the recesses for the headlamps. Using a sharp chisel recess the bumper to take the headlamps that are made from a contrasting colour timber, (I used Brazilian mahogany) or if you prefer use an offcut of timber and paint it red. Now radius off the ends and chamfer the top and bottom edges.

Now cut and fit all the other cross members to the chassis. For strength it's a good idea to both glue and screw these into position. At this stage cut and fit the three bearers that support the tipper bed, gluing and screwing them into the chassis.

2. The cab is not difficult to make. Mark out a pair of cab sides. To give an air of realism I have cut out the cab side windows, which also allows

small hands to get into the cab.

Cutting operations begin by removing the mudguard sections with a coping saw. Don't discard these pieces as they are later glued back in after shaping. With this section of the mudguard removed you can now make a start to cut the cab side windows. To make more of a feature of the door I decided to cut straight along the door line and around the window section. When the cutting is finished the window piece comes out and leaves a neat cut line which looks like a door. The other advantage of this method is that it gets the saw in and around the window and out at the end of the cut without having to drill starter holes for the blade etc.

Using glasspaper, work around the window edges and smooth things off and cut a rebate to accommodate the cab steps. Now back to the mudguard that has to be cut to allow the wheel to fit. Chamfer the top edge of the mudguard and glue it back on to the cab. All this amounts to a fair bit of work but the detail this adds to the finished model is well worth the effort.

3. The front of the cab has to be shaped. This curved section is best done with a plane or spokeshave to remove the bulk of wood, and finished off with a sandplate or glasspaper.

The actual radiator itself is made from a very thin piece of pine which is 'edged' by strips of Brazilian mahogany. The distinctive M A N lettering and lion are also made from mahogany and glued in place. Now make the seats, steering wheel, bunk bed, cab floor, roof and back.

4. Gluing the cab together is far easier if you have four wood cramps. Glue the sides to the floor and at the same time fit the back, front and roof. The cramps should be placed to hold the sides to the base which will steady the whole unit while the other pieces are attached. Do check that everything is square before the glue sets.

Once the glue has set, small steps are made and fitted to the cab sides in the recesses provided. Holes are now drilled for wing mirrors and plastic curtain wire is used to attach the mirrors to the cab. This wire is flexible and does not break when bumped which is inevitable when working in a sand pit.

5. The seats and bunk bed are now fitted. The dashboard is glued in place and the steering wheel fitted before the windscreen is put on.

6.   The perspex windscreen is cut to shape (a fine toothed saw and a very sharp plane work well on this material) and four holes drilled in the corners. Now the corresponding pilot holes in the cab should be slightly foreshortened, this will have the desired effect of bowing the windscreen when the screws are fitted. This curved windscreen is a prominent feature of the real truck and looks good on the model.

7.   Now although this is a tipper truck there is one great danger in actually making it tip. Children love sitting and standing on their toys and there is a very real chance that should a child sit on the tipper and get his or her fingers trapped it would be a very nasty accident. So to avoid any such dangers the tipper body is screwed down and a large opening tailgate allows sand and other rubble to be emptied.

8.   The floor, sides and ends of the tipper body are now cut and glued together. All tipper bodies have massive steel bracing for the sides. The bracing pieces are made from strips of timber. The hinged tipper flap is fitted using a length of piano hinge which is far stronger than separate hinges. The wooden dowels need to be chained to the sides of the body to prevent loss. They should be tapered so that a good push fit is achieved. Cup washers used under the screw heads that attach the chain to

the body and peg look very workmanlike.
The tipper body is secured to the chassis by screws that pass from the underside of cross member bearers up into the bottom of the tipper body.

9.   The fuel tank is shaped up from a block of wood and glued on top of the cross member that passes behind the front wheels.
The air reservoir tanks are shaped up from large diameter dowel rod and glued on the opposite side of the chassis from the fuel tank.

10.   The exhaust stack is shaped up from an offcut. The pipe itself must be plastic or rubber – don't be tempted to fit anything else otherwise it will scratch children's legs or arms. The plastic pipe is glued into the exhaust stack and in turn fitted on to the back of the cab.

11.   Now fit the axles. Before I fitted the wheels I painted the centres red – adding a dash of colour to the truck. It is necessary to fit lengths of plastic tube as spacers to keep the wheels off the chassis sides.

12.   A good finish is essential as this machine may well spend a good deal of time out of doors.

M A N 6-Wheel Tipper Truck Cutting List

Radiator Centre Panel	1 off 146 × 73 × 3mm (5¾ × 2⅞ × ⅛in) plywood
Radiator Edging	Make from 426 × 3 × 3mm (16¾ × ⅛ × ⅛in) timber
Letter and Motif	Make from 76 × 64 × 3mm (3 × 2½ × ⅛in) timber
Seat	2 off 133 × 54 × 51mm (5¼ × 2⅛ × 2in) timber
Exhaust	1 off 89 × 44 × 41mm (3½ × 1¾ × 1⅝in) timber
Air Cylinders	3 off 32mm (1¼in) × 22mm (⅞in) diam dowel
	1 off 51 × 35 × 20mm (2 × 1⅜ × ¾in) timber
Fuel Tank	1 off 76 × 76 × 44mm (3 × 3 × 1¾in) timber
Fuel Tank Support	1 off 184 × 32 × 20mm (7¼ × 1¼ × ¾in) timber
Mirror	2 off 60 × 35 × 12mm (2⅜ × 1⅜ × ½in) timber
Step	4 off 38 × 11 × 3mm (1½ × 7/16 × ⅛in) timber
Steering Wheel	1 off 35 × 35 × 6mm (1⅜ × 1⅜ × ¼in) timber
Steering Column	1 off 38mm (1½in) × 6mm (¼in) diam dowel
Body Support	3 off 273 × 38 × 20mm (10¾ × 1½ × ¾in) tanker
Dashboard	1 off 241 × 44 × 16mm (9½ × 1¾ × ⅝in) timber
Cab Floor	1 off 241 × 191 × 20mm (9½ × 7½ × ¾in) timber
Engine Cover	1 off 76 × 73 × 35mm (3 × 2⅞ × 1⅜) timber
Cab Rear Panel	1 off 241 × 165 × 20mm (9½ × 6½ × ¾in) timber
	1 off 241 × 41 × 12mm (9½ × 1⅝ × ½in) timber
Body Sides	2 off 422 × 152 × 20mm (16⅝ × 6 × ¾in) timber
Body Floor	1 off 422 × 208 × 20mm (16⅝ × 8¼ × ¾in) timber
Body Front Wall	1 off 248 × 191 × 20mm (9¾ × 7½ × ¾in) timber
	1 off 248 × 57 × 20mm (9¾ × 2¼ × ¾in) timber
Body Fixed Rear Panel	1 off 248 × 38 × 20mm (9¾ × 1½ × ¾in) timber
Body Hinged Rear Panel	1 off 248 × 114 × 20mm (9¾ × 4½ × ¾in) timber

M A N 6-Wheel Tipper Truck Cutting List *continued*

Body Reinforcing	2 off 422 × 35 × 12mm (16⅝ × 1⅜ × ½in) timber
	2 off 480 × 35 × 12mm (18⅞ × 1⅜ × ½in) timber
	6 off 82 × 35 × 12 (3¼ × 1⅜ × ½in) timber
	2 off 102 × 35 × 12mm (4 × 1⅜ × ½in) timber
	1 off 273 × 35 × 12mm (10¾ × 1⅜ × ½in) timber
Tailgate Pin	2 off 76mm (3in) × 9mm (⅜in) diam dowel
Cab Front Panel	1 off 279 × 114 × 16mm (11 × 4½ × ⅝in) timber
Front Bumper	1 off 279 × 57 × 20mm (11 × 2¼ × ¾in) timber
Headlights	2 off 41 × 20 × 3mm (1⅝ × ¾ × ⅛in) timber
Cab Roof	1 off 279 × 191 × 20mm (11 × 7½ × ¾in) timber
Cab Side Panel	2 off 295 × 191 × 20mm (11⅝ × 7½ × ¾in) timber
Chassis Member	2 off 673 × 111 × 20mm (26½ × 4⅜ × ¾in) timber
Cab Supports	2 off 241 × 41 × 20mm (9½ × 1⅝ × ¾in) timber
Rear Bumper	1 off 285 × 38 × 20mm (11¼ × 1½ × ¾in) timber
Ancillaries	10 off 152mm (6in) diam road wheels
	3 off 295mm (11⅝in) × 9mm (⅜in) diam steel axles
	2 off 41mm (1⅝in) long × 9mm (⅜in) i/diam spacer tubes
	6 off 9mm (⅜in) spring dome caps
	1 off 209mm (8½in) long × 20mm (¾in) o/diam plastic tube exhaust
	4 off 76mm (3in) long × 3mm (⅛in) diam soft wire mirror arms
	1 off 22mm (⅞in) long × 6mm (¼in) i/diam plastic tube steering column
	2 off 102mm (4in) lengths of chain – tail gate
	1 off 279 × 124 × 1.5mm (11 × 4⅞ × 1/16 in) clear plastic sheet – windscreen
	2 off 25mm (1in) brass hinges

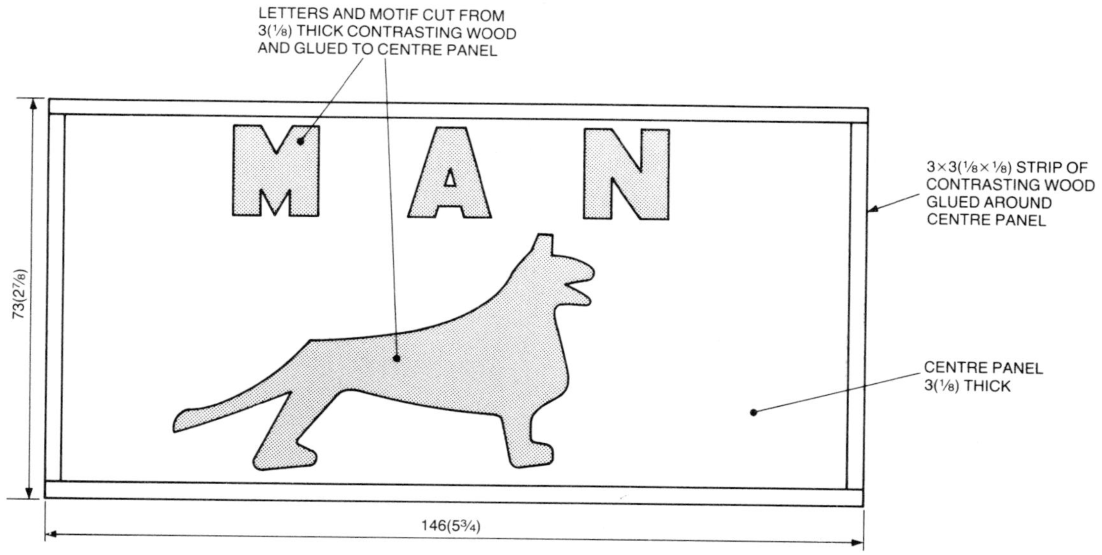
LETTERS AND MOTIF CUT FROM
3(⅛) THICK CONTRASTING WOOD
AND GLUED TO CENTRE PANEL
M A N
3×3(⅛×⅛) STRIP OF
CONTRASTING WOOD
GLUED AROUND
CENTRE PANEL
CENTRE PANEL
3(⅛) THICK
73(2⅞)
146(5¾)

RADIATOR DETAIL

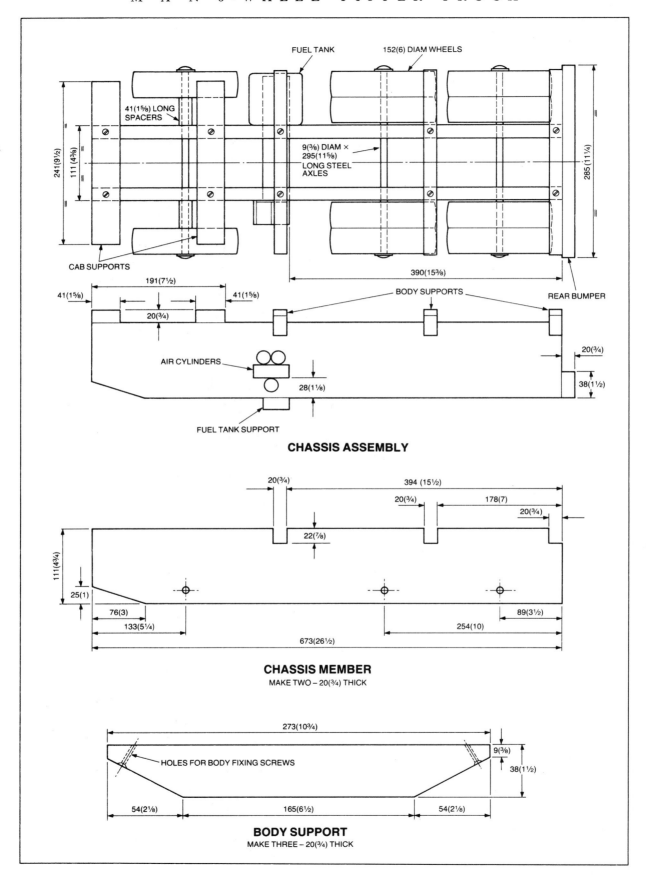

FUEL TANK

152(6) DIAM WHEELS

41(1⅝) LONG SPACERS

241(9½)

111(4⅜)

9(⅜) DIAM × 295(11⅝) LONG STEEL AXLES

285(11¼)

CAB SUPPORTS

390(15⅜)

191(7½)

41(1⅝)

41(1⅝)

20(¾)

BODY SUPPORTS

REAR BUMPER

AIR CYLINDERS

28(1⅛)

20(¾)

38(1½)

FUEL TANK SUPPORT

CHASSIS ASSEMBLY

20(¾)

394 (15½)

20(¾)

178(7)

20(¾)

22(⅞)

111(4¾)

25(1)

76(3)

133(5¼)

89(3½)

254(10)

673(26½)

CHASSIS MEMBER
MAKE TWO – 20(¾) THICK

273(10¾)

9(⅜)

HOLES FOR BODY FIXING SCREWS

38(1½)

54(2⅛)

165(6½)

54(2⅛)

BODY SUPPORT
MAKE THREE – 20(¾) THICK

106

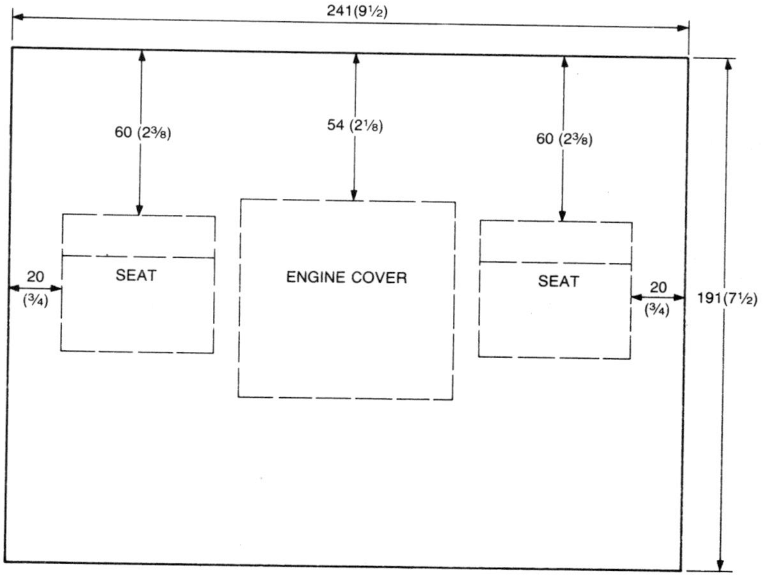

241(9½)
60 (2⅜)
54 (2⅛)
60 (2⅜)
20 (¾)
SEAT
ENGINE COVER
SEAT
20 (¾)
191(7½)

CAB FLOOR 20 (¾) THICK

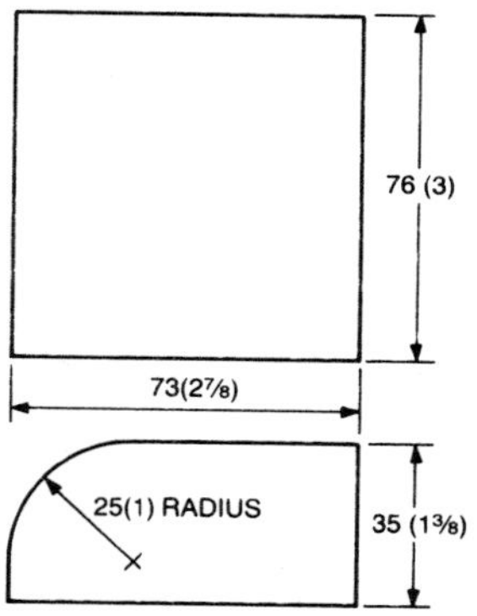

76 (3)
73(2⅞)
25(1) RADIUS
35 (1⅜)

ENGINE COVER

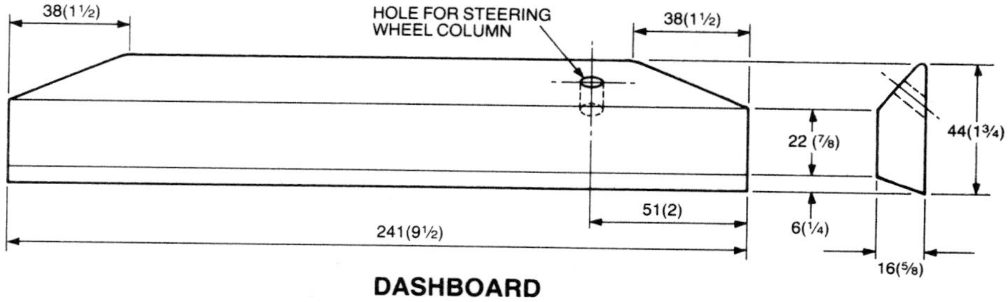

38(1½)
HOLE FOR STEERING WHEEL COLUMN
38(1½)
22 (⅞)
44(1¾)
51(2)
241(9½)
6(¼)
16(⅝)

DASHBOARD

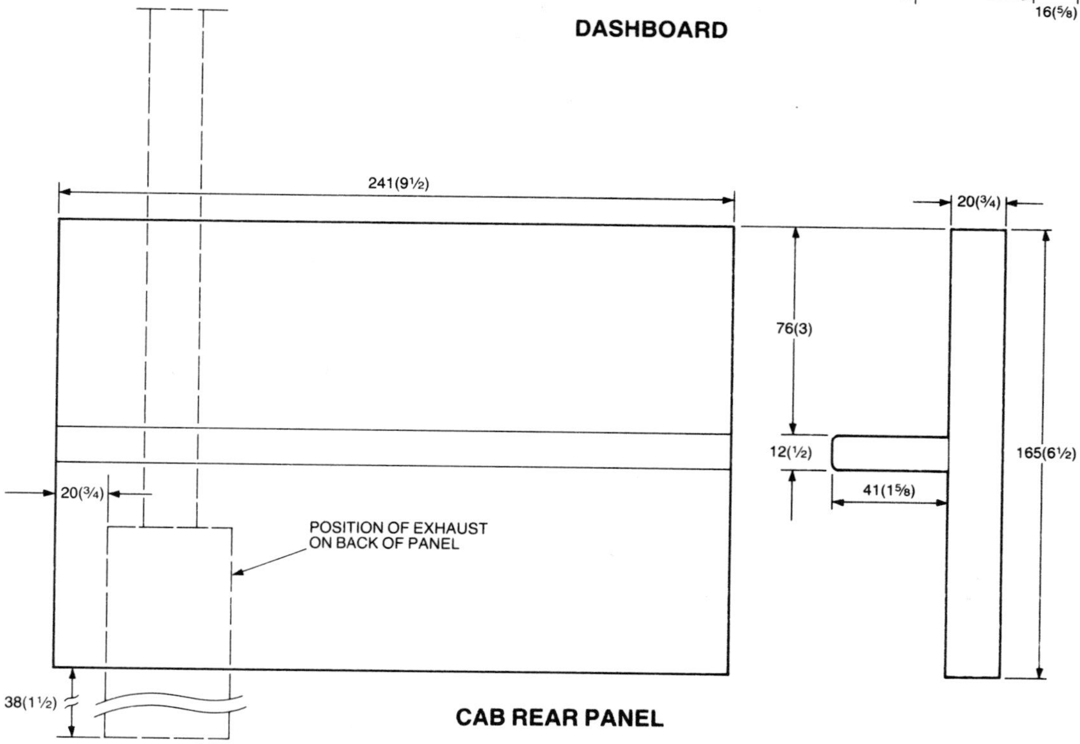

241(9½)
20(¾)
76(3)
12(½)
165(6½)
41(1⅝)
20(¾)
POSITION OF EXHAUST ON BACK OF PANEL
38(1½)

CAB REAR PANEL

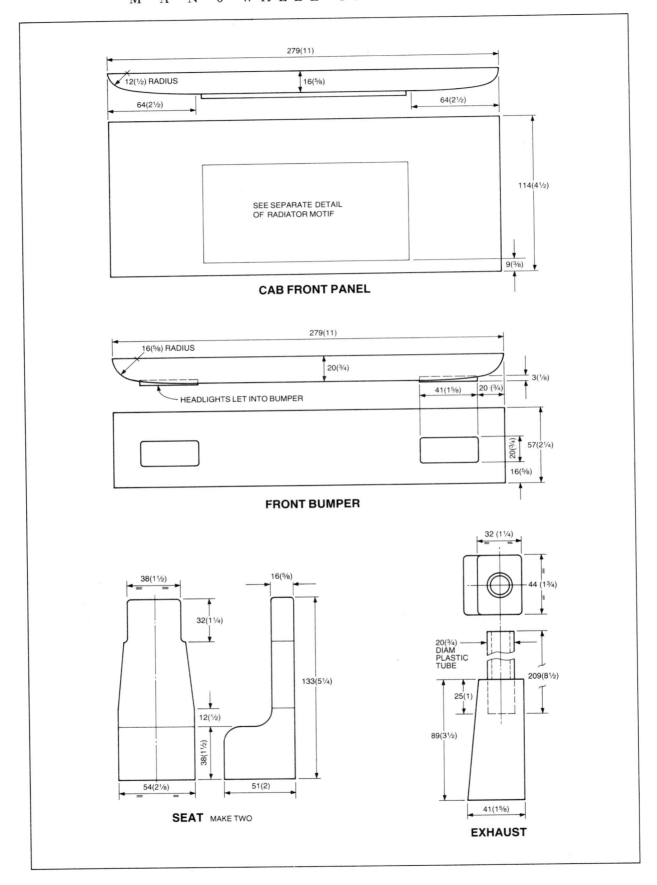

279(11)

12(½) RADIUS

16(⅝)

64(2½)

64(2½)

114(4½)

SEE SEPARATE DETAIL
OF RADIATOR MOTIF

9(⅜)

CAB FRONT PANEL

279(11)

16(⅝) RADIUS

20(¾)

3(⅛)

HEADLIGHTS LET INTO BUMPER

41(1⅝)

20 (¾)

20(¾)

57(2¼)

16(⅝)

FRONT BUMPER

38(1½)

16(⅝)

32(1¼)

32(1¼)

44 (1¾)

133(5¼)

20(¾)
DIAM
PLASTIC
TUBE

12(½)

209(8½)

38(1½)

25(1)

54(2⅛)

51(2)

89(3½)

41(1⅝)

SEAT MAKE TWO

EXHAUST

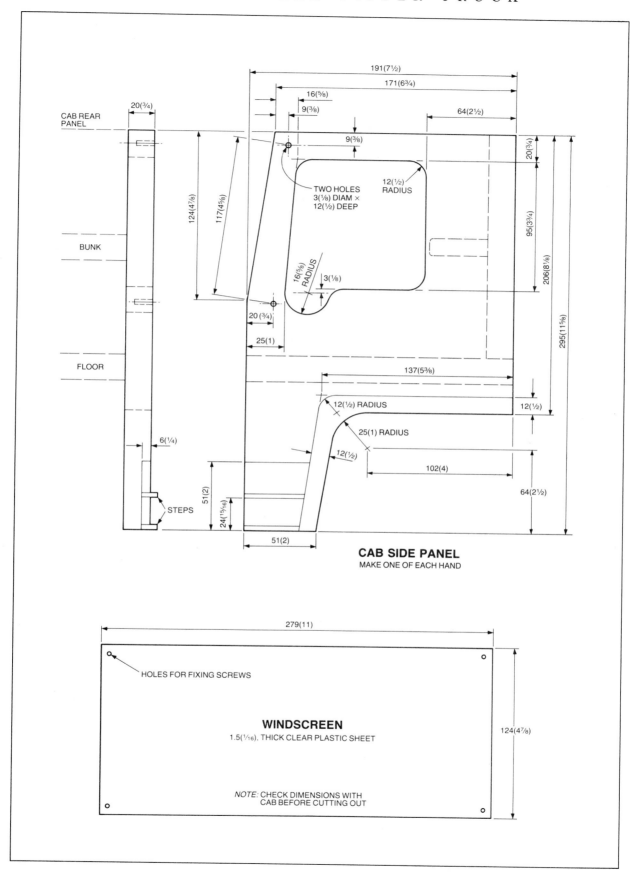

CAB REAR PANEL

BUNK

FLOOR

STEPS

TWO HOLES
3(⅛) DIAM ×
12(½) DEEP

16(⅝)
RADIUS

12(½)
RADIUS

12(½) RADIUS

25(1) RADIUS

CAB SIDE PANEL
MAKE ONE OF EACH HAND

HOLES FOR FIXING SCREWS

WINDSCREEN
1.5(¹⁄₁₆), THICK CLEAR PLASTIC SHEET

NOTE: CHECK DIMENSIONS WITH
CAB BEFORE CUTTING OUT

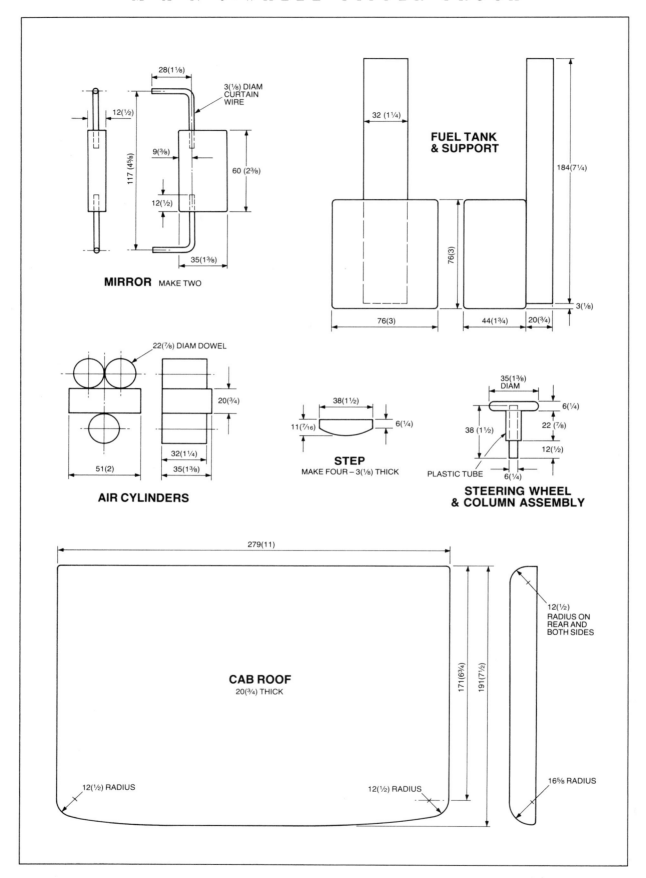

MIRROR MAKE TWO

28(1⅛)

3(⅛) DIAM CURTAIN WIRE

12(½)

117 (4⅝)

9(⅜)

60 (2⅜)

12(½)

35(1⅜)

FUEL TANK & SUPPORT

32 (1¼)

184(7¼)

76(3)

76(3)

44(1¾)

20(¾)

3(⅛)

22(⅞) DIAM DOWEL

20(¾)

51(2)

32(1¼)

35(1⅜)

AIR CYLINDERS

38(1½)

11(⁷⁄₁₆)

6(¼)

STEP
MAKE FOUR – 3(⅛) THICK

35(1⅜) DIAM

6(¼)

38 (1½)

22 (⅞)

12(½)

PLASTIC TUBE

6(¼)

STEERING WHEEL & COLUMN ASSEMBLY

279(11)

12(½) RADIUS ON REAR AND BOTH SIDES

171(6¾)

191(7½)

CAB ROOF
20(¾) THICK

12(½) RADIUS

12(½) RADIUS

16⅝ RADIUS

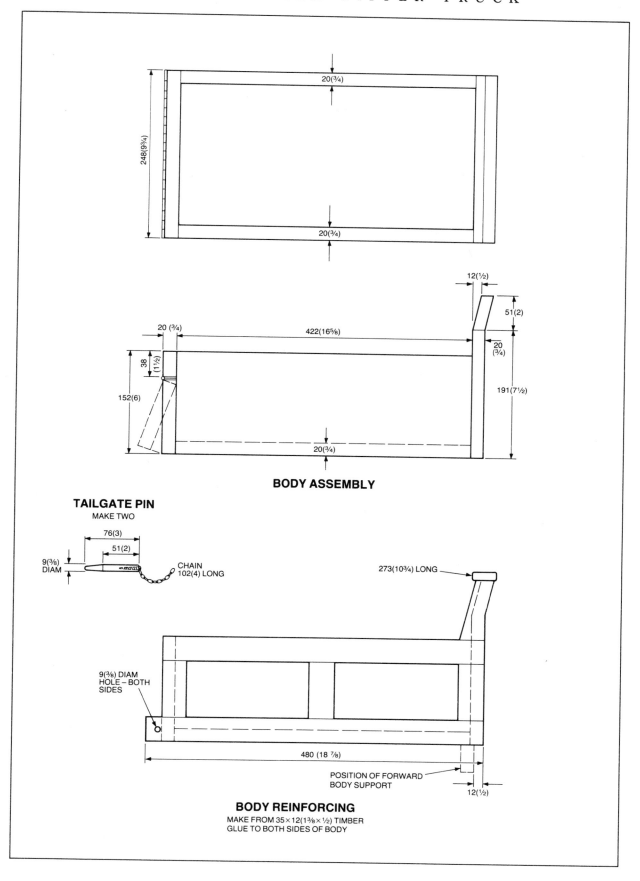

20(¾)

248(9¾)

20(¾)

12(½)

51(2)

20 (¾)

422(16⅝)

20
(¾)

38
(1½)

152(6)

191(7½)

20(¾)

BODY ASSEMBLY

TAILGATE PIN
MAKE TWO

76(3)

51(2)

9(⅜)
DIAM

CHAIN
102(4) LONG

273(10¾) LONG

9(⅜) DIAM
HOLE – BOTH
SIDES

480 (18 ⅞)

POSITION OF FORWARD
BODY SUPPORT

12(½)

BODY REINFORCING
MAKE FROM 35×12(1⅜×½) TIMBER
GLUE TO BOTH SIDES OF BODY

TIMBER FOR TOYS – A FEW SIMPLE TIPS FOR SUCCESS

Peter Grimsdale – Director, Swedish Finnish Timber
Council

This book is full of ideas for the use of timber, projects suited for everyone from the novice to the experienced. The one thing all the projects have in common is that they are made predominantly from timber. Now, depending upon your level of skill and the project you choose, you will probably spend many hours making and finishing your project and perhaps give it to someone you love. A few simple tips on buying your timber will ensure that your cherished gift remains in tip-top condition for many years to come.

Down to Basics

The majority of the projects in this book are made from softwoods and before you go out to buy your timber it is as well to have some knowledge of the difference beween softwoods and hardwoods and their relative merits.

The terms softwood and hardwood are often misunderstood. Broadly speaking, softwoods come from any trees bearing cones and needles (firs and pines), hardwoods come from all other trees (oak, mahogany, beech, teak etc). The terms hardwood and softwood can be misleading since not all hardwoods are hard and durable any more than all softwoods are soft and non-durable.

For DIY toy making, softwoods are eminently suitable since they are reasonably inexpensive, easy to work with hand tools, readily available in a wide range of sizes and can be finished by hand to a very high standard.

Hardwoods for the handyman are expensive and often difficult to obtain and work without specialized tools. However, because they are often very beautiful they are frequently used in toy making in small items where a contrast is needed to the more uniform colour of most softwoods, for example, headlights on motor cars etc.

Choosing Softwoods

The vast majority of softwood sold in this country is imported and certainly it is only the imported material which is likely to be consistently good enough for toy making. Of all the softwood which we import around 50 per cent comes from Sweden and Finland. If one excludes the lower qualities, then the Nordic supply is an even greater proportion of our imports.

As a result of this large market share and the widespread distribution of Nordic timbers, probably 75 per cent of the quality softwoods you will find in your local timber merchant or DIY store started in the forests of Sweden and Finland.

The most common softwood available in the UK is European Redwood, also known variously by names which may be more familiar to you such as deal, redwood, pine and knotty pine (for the lower qualities of wall panelling). Redwood is characterised by the slight colour difference between the timber at the centre of the tree (heartwood) and the narrow band of lighter wood towards the outside (sapwood), hence the distinctive light reddish bands apparent in wider sections. When used indoors, clear varnished or left unfinished, Redwood tends to darken, mellowing with age to a rich golden hue.

Sweden and Finland also export European Whitewood to the UK and this is often sold by timber merchants under various names such as whitewood, white pine, spruce or white deal. It is used extensively for building purposes and is distinguishable from Redwood by its more uniform, whiter colour. Whitewood is a little harder to work with hand tools than Redwood. For this reason Redwood is preferred for toy making.

Timber quality

Nordic Redwood is graded by appearance, freedom from knots and other natural features. This system of grading has been devised to ease trading between Nordic sawmills and UK timber importers. To a large extent these commercial gradings are not relevant to the toy maker.

The best way for handymen to select timber is to find a friendly, local supplier and explain to him what the timber is required for. Ask to have a look at the timber available – any reasonable supplier will accommodate you – if not go elsewhere.

Always check each board for defects, such as splits or loose knots. Providing that the timber looks alright then it probably is, assuming that it is in good, dry condition. If you do not want to be disappointed do not order timber by telephone.

Moisture condition

Virtually all Nordic softwoods are carefully kiln-dried before being sent to the UK. If buying timber from other sources always ask your supplier if the timber has been kiln-dried. If the timber has been kept covered in this country then it should be suitable for your purposes.

When timber is wetted for prolonged periods it swells, shrinking again as it dries out. This movement can cause splitting and cupping in wider boards. Therefore, if the timber has been allowed to get wet by improper storage, it probably is not suitable for making toys.

As a rough on-the-spot moisture check, if it looks, smells or feels wet to the touch then it probably is unsuitable, so don't buy it.

No matter how carefully controlled the moisture content of the timber has been it is a certainty that the timber will dry even further when taken into your centrally heated home. It is a wise precaution to let the timber stand in your home for a few days before you begin to make your toys.

Timber sizes

Timber from Sweden and Finland is sawn to British Standard sizes and in metric thicknesses, widths and lengths. There are a wide variety of sizes available and most of the projects in this book are designed around a number of these standard sizes — thus reducing the amount of re-sizing which you need to do.

When buying timber, remember that although sizes are given as say 25mm × 50mm par (planed all round), planing will remove 3 to 5mm so that the actual size may be only 20mm × 45mm.

Since different planers tend to machine to slightly different sizes it is advisable to buy all of your timber at the same time and from the same source.

If you need to have timber planed to a precise dimension then you can usually save yourself many hours of hard work by asking your timber merchant to do this for you. It may add 20 to 25 per cent to your timber costs.

Timber is sold in metric lengths and in 300mm increments. Do be sure when you order timber that if you have it cut to length, both you and the merchant know precisely what you are expecting. For example, the nearest metric length to 8 feet is 2.4m (7ft 10½in). Watch this if you really need 8 feet.

Wooden toys are forever

Armed with these few simple rules you can be your own timber expert next time you visit your local supplier. Avoiding the simplest pitfalls will mean that you can use this most versatile and beautiful of all raw materials in toys that will last you and your family a lifetime. Happy modelling!

USEFUL ADDRESSES

ACCESSORIES
You may experience difficulty in obtaining the right types of wheels, water pumps and valves featured on toys and models in this book. If so write for information enclosing S A E to: R Blizzard (Wheels), P O Box 5, Gloucester GL3 4RJ (UK)

Publications and Catalogues
Practical Woodworking — published monthly and available from newsagents, it includes not only a wealth of articles but suppliers of goods relating to all aspects of woodworking.

Woodworker — published monthly and available from newsagents, it provides wealth of information on all woodworking techniques.

The Swedish Finnish Timber Council, 21-25 Carolgate, Retford, Notts, DN22 6BZ. Send a large S A E for free D I Y leaflets on a range of woodworking projects.

AEG Power Tools – their catalogue lists a fine range of hand power tools and bench mounted machines. Send a large S A E to: AEG, 217 Bath Road, Slough SL1 4AW.

Stanley Tools. A huge catalogue full of fascinating tools, chisels, tapes, screwdrivers etc. Send a large S A E to: The Stanley Works Ltd., Woodside, Sheffield S3 9PD.

Robert Bosch Ltd (John Roberts or Tony Merritt) P.O. Box 99, Broad Water Park, North Orbital Road, Denham, Middlesex. Bosch carry a fine selection of electric power tools.

John Boddy's Fine Wood and Tool Store Ltd, Dept PW, Riverside Sawmills, Boroughbridge, N. Yorkshire YO5 9LJ. For tools, timbers and all woodworking supplies.